THE LAST MINYAN IN Havana

Copyright© 2000

by

Betty Heisler-Samuels

Published by

Chutzpah Publishing

19355 NE 36 Ct. #21K

Aventura, FL 33180

IBSN 0-9703078-0-2

Library of Congress Card Number: 00-106497

We shall not cease from exploration

And the end of all our exploring

Will be to arrive where we started

And know the place for the first time.

T.S. Elliot

To my father, who loved life

and my mother, who nurtured it

and to a whole generation who

created and lost their own piece of paradise

in a beautiful, betrayed land.

THE LAST MINYAN IN Havana

Betty Heisler-Samuels

CONTENTS

PREFACE

In January of 1994 I came back to Cuba. More than thirty three years had gone by since I took one of the last Pan Am flights that left the island before relations with the U.S. were broken.

The minute we landed at Jose Marti International Airport memories came rushing in... of my home, my school, our beach club, the place where I was first kissed. Having lived the first nineteen years of my life in Cuba I had the opportunity to experience a great deal of the magic of that land. A land that forever marked me with a special sensitivity to certain sights and sounds that I had tried to suppress during all these years, simply because it was too painful to remember. The sight of narrow cobblestone streets, of wrought-iron balconies crowded together, or of a perfect blue sky; the sound of waves crashing against the walls of the Malecon, their spray creating a salty mist all around.

What I was not prepared to see was the painful decay of the city that had once been hailed as the Paris of the Caribbean. Buildings that had not received a coat of paint in thirty years, balconies being propped up with wooden sticks, department stores with bicycle tires as their only window display.

Jewish life in Cuba lasted less than fifty years, but it was intense and historically significant, since, due to its strategic geographical location, the island acted as a springboard to freedom for many refugees during World War II. The few Jews that remained on the island now were either old and terribly neglected, or young and dispirited for lack of work.

El Patronato, the big synagogue that was built at the height of the Batista regime, was fading fast, its once proud *bima* now filled with tattered chairs, the ceiling falling by pieces.

Interestingly enough, I found out that Jewishness was going through a renaissance, as many people, disenchanted with the ideals of a revolution that they felt had betrayed them, went looking for something to believe in, a new spiritual purpose that religion seemed to fulfill. We were welcomed at the Patronato with a Shabbat dinner and Israeli dances. Most of the young performers had only one Jewish parent. They had embraced Jewishness with a new fervor, and even though they had no rabbi, they received Jewish instruction from a visiting *sheliaj* from Mexico that came to the island periodically. One had the feeling that this was the only thing they were clinging to, in the midst of their mounting despair. I came back exhilarated from the trip, but heartbroken.

In March of 1999 I took my daughter back for a look at the country were her father and I were born. To my surprise, this time I saw new five-star hotels springing up amidst the remains of once staid buildings gone ragged around the edges and luxury apartments being snapped up by well-heeled European businessmen at exorbitant prices. The Cuban people are still suffering the austerity of the special period that started with the disenfranchising from the former Soviet Union. But despite the U.S. embargo, the rest of the world has discovered Cuba; and French, German, Italian, Spanish and English tourists crowd the outdoor cafes in the newly restored sections of Old Havana as an occasional cruise ship docks in the harbor.

When I visited the Patronato, the old synagogue was still in shambles, but most of it has since been restored with funds raised by exiled Cuban Jews and the Joint Distribution Committee. We visited our old home and were greeted warmly by perfect strangers that did not hesitate to share their tales of misery with us. A young woman was still waiting for a permit to join her husband who had emigrated to the U.S. five years earlier. Her permit had now to be obtained through a national lottery and years of longing made her young, pretty face look a lot older than her years. We took a picture together in my old bedroom, where I had slept as a teenager and she now shared with her mother. The apartment, in fact, had been cut in two, and her brother and her sister-in-law lived in the other half, which had been sealed by a wall.

As long as Castro is in power it is hard to imagine Cuba having a complete renaissance, and nobody can guess how long that will take, but it is difficult, if not impossible, to keep a secret like this hidden for too long. One thing is certain... the bubble has already started to rise to the surface.

INTRODUCTION

The first Jewish presence in Cuba goes back to Christopher Columbus, who took many conversos and Jews fleeing the Spanish Inquisition on his first voyages to the New World. One of them, Columbus' interpreter Luis de Torres, spoke Hebrew, Aramaic and Arabic besides Spanish. It was de Torres who first documented the custom of cigar smoking, reporting having seen "many people, women as well as men with a flaming stick of herb in their hand, taking in its aromatic smell from time to time". Columbus continued his voyage northward, but de Torres preferred to stay in Cuba, where he became the representative of the Royal Spanish government until his death several years later.

Jews came to Cuba during the first years of Spanish rule and by 1516 the presence of conversos so alarmed the Church that a bishop sent a letter to Madrid complaining that "practically every ship docking in Havana is filled with Hebrews and New Christians." By 1520 the Santo Oficio set up headquarters in

Cuba and Francisco Lopez de Leon was the first Jew to be executed for Judaizing, his fortune of 150,000 pesos confiscated by the Catholic Church. The Inquisition continued its efforts and many others were burned at the stake until the early part of the eighteenth century.

Because of its strategic location at the gate of the Americas, Cuba became the cornerstone of Spain's colonial economic system, Havana's natural harbor acting as the convening point for the Spanish flotilla before going back to Europe. This was a fact that did not escape the attention of Britain, which waged war against Spain for the conquest of Cuba and for a brief period, exactly ten months in 1762, Cuba was ruled by the British, who brought free enterprise and the development of big-scale agriculture to the island. Jacob Franks, a New York Jewish businessman, was supplier to the British troops in Jamaica and in 1762 members of his firm together with Jews from Martinique and Guadeloupe helped abolish the Spanish monopolist system and established trade links with the Jewish houses in Kingston, Curacao, London, Amsterdam, Hamburg and New York, opening up new trade avenues to the insofar isolated island.

The Spanish returned to Cuba after the Treaty of Paris but the Jews who came with the British remained. And most importantly, the economic system instituted by the British was retained. By 1763 twenty Jewish men lived in Havana. The Cuban sugar industry, developed by Hernando de Castro, became the biggest and most mechanized in the world, utilizing steam-powered mills and narrow gauge railroads. Expanding *ingenios* (sugar mills) dominated the landscape from Havana to Puerto Principe and by 1860 Cuba produced

INTRODUCTION

500,000 tons of sugar annually, nearly one third of the world's production. The sugar revolution created a new wealthy class of plantation owners and a new middle class of merchants. Some of both were Jews.

The booming Cuban economy brought an end to the Spanish domination of the island and the beginning of a new relationship between Cuba and the United States. By 1895 Cuba's political and economic conflict with Spain grew more severe. As more and more Americans invested in their neighbor to the South, U.S. investments in Cuba reached $50,000,000 and annual trade with Cuba averaged about $100,000,000.

Cuban political movements were organized by exiles in the United States and were coordinated by Cuban national hero Jose Marti in New York and Tampa. Marti equated Cuban suffering under Spanish rule with Jewish suffering at the hands of the Santo Oficio. His advisor was a Jew by the name of Joseph Steinberg. Steinberg and his brothers Max and Edward organized the fundraising arm of the Cuban revolution, giving Marti his first financing. Don Tomas Estrada Palma, then delegate plenipotentiary to the Cuban Revolution and later Cuba's first president, appointed Steinberg "Captain of the Army of Liberation" and authorized him to solicit and collect monies in Cuba and abroad.

War between Cuba and Spain broke out on February 24, 1895. Three years later the United States declared war against Spain, and more than four thousand American Jews participated in that conflict. The first Jewish cemetery was established in Cuba in order to bury the American Jewish soldiers who died in that war. Some of the American soldiers that came to fight the Spanish-American War remained in Cuba, creating the beginnings of the American Jewish community, which in turn founded the United Hebrew Congregation in 1906. Over the years American Jews did not mix much with the rest of the Jews and remained the wealthiest segment of the Jewish population on the island.

Sephardic Jews started coming in from Turkey around 1902, but their numbers did not become significant until 1908, after the abortive revolt against the Ottoman Sultan. Others came from Syria, North Africa and other areas of the Mediterranean, some escaping the onset of World War I. Most were humble, mostly uneducated and poor. Even though the United Hebrew Congregation offered them limited assistance, they never really welcomed the Sephardim, with whom they had little or nothing in common. This led to the formation of the Union Hebrea Shevet Ahim, the Sephardic Congregation, in 1914.

By 1920 the Cuban Jewish community was polarized into two groups: the affluent, educated American Jews and the more provincial Sephardim. Both were beginning to reap the benefits of the economic expansion that followed World War I. But in 1921 a new law passed in the U.S. Congress changed the future of the small Cuban Jewish community. Emigration quotas were established for Eastern European countries. No longer could people emigrate freely into North America. Cuba became an attractive alternative since visas were not needed to come to the island. Moreover, the United States accepted the new immigrants after a one-year stay in Cuba.

Large numbers of Eastern European Jews began arriving in Cuba in 1921. They came mostly from the *shtetls* of Poland and Russia and their manner of dress and behavior left a lot to be desired. The newcomers had also gone through the experience of war, German occupation and the Russian Revolution. Noisy and dissatisfied, they had a revolutionary outlook. Cuba's American Jews on the other hand were preoccupied with their flourishing businesses and preferred reasonableness and respectability. They regarded the immigrants as poor relations.

Notwithstanding their humble background, from the moment of their arrival Eastern European Jews became a vital part of the Jewish community, creating their own multiple organizations. The religiously observant founded the Orthodox Congregation Adath Israel in 1921, and those who favored debates and cultural activities met daily at the *Yidishe Kulturgrupe* in Havana's Parque Central. The *Yidishe Kultur Tsenter* offered an evening school with Spanish and English courses, literary lectures, debates and an amateur theater. But it was a left-wing organization and formed close ties with the Cuban labor movement, setting itself apart from members of the *bourgeois*. This attitude antagonized the United Hebrew Congregation, which eventually caused its demise. The Centro Isrelita took its place shortly after, meeting the financial, cultural and educational needs of Cuban Jews.

The *Yidishe Cultur Tsenter* quickly reorganized under the name of the *Kultur Farain*, and became the Soviet Union's chief unofficial spokesman in the island, where it financed the publication and distribution of communist propaganda. Ironically, many of these same European Jews who started as devoted communists, managed over the years to amass a considerable fortune in Cuba, only to have it taken away by people who shared their early ideology once Castro's revolution came to power.

1

AZABACHES AND AVE MARIAS

I was born where palm trees curtsy to morning breezes and stars display their fire on a sheath of velvet in the evening sky. In this tropical paradise my earliest memories are of a pair of strong arms lifting me up, up up into the air... until I was high enough to catch in my face the full warmth of the morning sun. That warmth and that breeze were to become forever embedded in my memory, the first taste of bliss that to this day I always associate with the caress of the sun on my cheeks.

Little did I know then that those arms had felt unmerciful cold before holding me and that the man they belonged to, my father, had his own share of memories from another place and another time, far different and a lot less pleasant than the ones we shared on that peaceful day. But at the age of three nothing could intrude in my little perfect world— and so my story starts

The Havana of my childhood belongs to the 1940's and is peopled with dark-haired women clad in snug silk crepe dresses, their hair piled up in trendy bouffant updos and men dressed in linen suits and guayaberas, the dressy linen shirt-suit of the tropics, their hair slicked back with Vaseline in the style immortalized by Valentino. We lived in Aguacate, a small town two hours away by train from the city. There my father ran a general store that my maternal grandfather had opened for him when he married my mother.

My parents took me to Aguacate right from the big Havana hospital where my mother went to give birth, and from the moment of my arrival I found a very special place in the heart of Doña Dominga. The owner of the only restaurant in town had grown children of her own and became overwhelmed at the sight of the tiny blonde baby girl, so different from all the other babies in Aguacate. To say that she took me under her wing is an understatement. She used to send one of her sons for me every morning and, before the maid had a chance to change my clothes, she used to spirit me away into her kitchen and feed me freshly-laid farm eggs fried to perfection in country butter (she used to keep a hen just for me) and freshly-squeezed orange juice. Afterwards she used to walk me back to my home and by the time my mother woke up and tried to feed me I did not want to eat any more. For years my mother would lament that I had no appetite in the mornings and did not know how I managed to stay alive until lunch after not eating a thing all night.

The Dominica became my den. It was there that I sat in the cane-backed chairs hardly reaching the marble-topped cafe tables that were scattered throughout the Victorian structure, its high-beamed ceilings echoing the arches of a turn-of-the-century country palace. Only this one was peopled with the intelligentsia of the town: the doctor, the druggist and even the barber, as well as the *colonos* that farmed the nearby countryside.

All would come to the Dominica for their morning *cafe con leche*, served with crusty Cuban bread and fresh country butter. As for me, I hung around for the *capuchinos*, the cone-shaped sweets soaked in syrup that the baker of the Dominica baked every morning. The first batch, of course, was served to me. I would eat one and then Doña Dominga would take the rest to our house where later we would feast on the sugary confections, that we kept ice cold in the ice box.

Cuba was a magical land that sometimes enveloped us in an otherworldly mantle of unexplained experiences. One day my mother was entertaining a friend from Havana when I started to cry. She picked me up and put me to her breast, whereupon I started to feed contentedly. A peasant woman who had recently given birth herself asked for permission to come into the back of the store in order to use the rest room. She took one look at me and told my mother: "Look how good she feeds!".

Shortly after she left I'm told that I developed a sudden fever and sunk into a very deep sleep. Alarmed, my mother sent for Doña Dominga. "That woman gave the child the evil eye," said Doña Dominga upon hearing what had happened and came back a few minutes later with a rosary in hand. "I will pray one Padre Nuestro and two Ave Marias," she announced and proceeded to pray fervently as she fingered the beads. Fifteen minutes later the fever subsided and I opened my eyes.

I guess we will never know how the fever started or how it went away, but Doña Dominga's rosary stayed in her apron from then on. "Paulina," she told my mother before she left, "this girl needs an *azabache*," and the next day she came in with an onyx bead set in gold that from that day on I wore pinned to my underclothes to ward off the evil eye.

In addition to prayers and *azabaches*, there was a whole list of herbs that were used for whatever ailed you —probably brought in by the Chinese that came to Cuba to build the railroads. If you became really sick, you could always call the doctor, but for everyday's aches and pains the druggist could dispense your favorite herb. There was star anise for babies' colics, chamomile for stomach upset and cinnamon for a delayed period. You would brew each herb and drink the concoction that at least most of the time tasted pretty good and more often than not took care of the immediate problem.

As in all the islands, but to a lesser extent than in the rest of the Caribbean, the blacks played an important part in Cuban society. They came as slaves to work the sugar plantations, mostly from the Congo, and brought their own rituals with them to the new world. But unlike the British in North America, the Spaniards who ruled the island thought nothing of consorting with their black slaves. As a result most colonial households were populated with a retinue of mulattos who were readily accepted into the fold. Cuban blacks and the growing population of half-breeds grew up with little resentment towards their masters, and once slavery was abolished were readily accepted into society. If not into the high classes, at least into the lower echelons, where they intermingled freely with the whites and the Chinese creating a breed of mestizos unique to the island. In time, some of these half-breeds came into positions of power such as the one held by Batista, a self-educated mestizo who ruled Cuba in two different historically significant periods of time, first as Army Chief during the 30's and later as president until deposed by Castro. The blacks brought with them their music, their colorful folklore, and their religion, which in time became an integral part of Cuban culture in addition to the traditional observance of Catholicism.

Sometimes while walking down the street, I would see a black man or woman completely dressed in white. Tomasa, the black cook of the Dominica, explained that they had made a promise to the deity and they had to dress that way until whatever they asked for came true. The blacks prayed to Chango and Yemaya, two deities they had brought in from Africa. In Cuba, Chango was personified in the image of Santa Barbara. Most other people were devotees of the Caridad del Cobre, a black virgin that legend has it appeared to two fishermen who were lost at sea, one black and one white, bringing them safely back to shore. Pictures of the black virgin, with her shining black face and beautiful robe floating over the two seamen in their small boat could be seen everywhere. Over the years Chango and Yemaya, as well as the Caridad del Cobre, which became the patron saint of Cuba, were infused with the figure of the Virgin Mary, and revered in altars throughout the country by blacks and whites alike.

One day I refused to eat Doña Dominga's eggs. Usually they were orangey-red and soft and gooey, the way I liked them, but that particular morning they were dry and overdone. Without delay Doña Dominga summoned Tomasa, who came in from behind the huge coal stove in front of which she spent most of the day, and started crying with big, deep sobs. Tears were rolling down her round brown cheeks and fell on the neckline of her white cotton dress until it got so wet that Doña Dominga took her aside.

"What's wrong, Tomasa, are you sick, is your husband all right?"
"No, Doña Dominga, I am not sick, but my husband is not all right," she said. *And the howling starting all over again, only stronger this time.*

It turned out that José, Tomasa's husband of six months, had gotten involved with a young girl in town and wasn't coming home evenings any more. Doña Dominga pondered this confession for a moment and then, probably thinking of the danger of losing both her cook and her restaurant, came up with a radical solution. "Take off your apron and grab your purse, you're coming to town with me," she commanded and off went Tomasa and Doña Dominga into the next bus to Havana and did not show up until the last bus rolled back into Aguacate. That evening Tomasa went home with a bag full of herbs and the next day she was back behind the coal stove as happy as a well-fed puppy.

"Well, how did it go?" asked Doña Dominga, stepping gingerly into the kitchen the following morning as she placed a plate of eggs that Tomasa handed her, right in front of me. I looked at both of them without understanding what was going on, hesitantly put the first bite into my mouth, and then grinned and swallowed with delight. All I knew was that my eggs were as good as ever. The white crispy and brown and the yolk running just so.

"José is back home," was all Tomasa said, her brown hands busily squeezing oranges for my juice, but her smile said it all.

What I didn't know then is that Doña Dominga had taken Tomasa to a babalao, an Afro-Cuban shaman who practiced black magic. He had given Tomasa a recipe for a potion that she had to brew with a variety of herbs and some other less orthodox ingredients. That night she gave it to José as soon as he came through the door on the pretext that he was catching a cold and the rest, as they say, is history. José never strayed again and him and Tomasa had four children over the thirty years they were together until he succumbed to a bad fit of pneumonia. During all those years, once a month Tomasa would board the early bus to Havana and she would step down in Aguacate at the end of the day with an armful of herbs. And I knew that whenever I showed up at the Dominica after one of those trips my eggs were going to be better than ever!

With so much ritual around us, it was a miracle that we stuck to our Judaism, or perhaps because of that we realized that we had to make a concerted effort to stay within the fold. Women of my mother's generation straddled two cultures. Most of them came to Cuba very young —my mother was only seven— and were raised with the structure and values of Europe, but they readily opened up to the warmth and sensuality of their adopted tropical country like flowers to the sun. They reveled in the friendliness and openness of the Cuban people who, especially in the less sophisticated country towns, took them in as family and made them part of small-town society, but as seductive as this lifestyle was, they knew they had to become part of the *kehila*, the group that had been the keystone of life in the *shtetl* in order to raise their children in a Jewish way.

My mother missed her family and the big city and by the time I was three she persuaded my father to move back to Havana, where we settled in with my grandparents. My grandfather Maximo opened a bigger store for my father to run. This time in El Cerro, a city at the very limits of Havana, beyond which laid the mostly undeveloped areas that later would become the suburbs of Marianao and Miramar. The store was right on the Calzada, in front of the street-car depot and I spent many an afternoon watching the comings and goings of the cable cars.

When my grandparents entertained, which was often, my grandmother used to peek into my room and I, pretending to be still asleep, would hear her refer to me as "her jewel" to her admiring friends. These were often the last words I would hear before falling asleep, a lullaby to sweeten my dreams. On nights when my grandparents did not entertain, I was rocked to sleep in the arms of my Abuela Sara, who would sit in the cozy living room of her Cerro apartment, in a big wood and cane rocking chair and lull me to sleep to the tune of *roshinkas mit mandlen*. I did not learn the meaning of the words until much later, but to this day that melody still delivers a generous dose of well being to my soul.

If my grandmother took care of my physical comforts, it was my grandfather Maximo who expanded my young mind. From him I heard for the first time about the old country, the mythical *Lita* that he still remembered with love and I learned how he used to take my mother ice skating in the lake as a child, something that to me seemed totally fantastic, living where I lived. The sight of an icy lake and shiny metal skates became one of the fantasies that spurred my young imagination at the time.

There was another member of our family with whom I had a very special relationship. My uncle Eli lived with my grandparents and from what I gather must have been the black sheep of the family. He was a handsome, charming man, but never got married, preferring instead to bask in the warmth of our

tight little household. Many years later I heard that he had gotten involved with a Cuban woman, a beautiful half-breed
whom we never met, since he would have never insulted my
grandfather by marrying a non-Jew. Instead we became his
family and me being his only great-niece, he would dream
up ways to entertain me, always throwing in a little fun
for himself.

I could not have been much older than three when uncle Eli
and I started sneaking out every afternoon to the corner cafe.
El Cafe de los Chinos was run by a Chinese family that made
their own ice cream using the tropical fruits that were in season, and it became a popular meeting place for the people of
the neighborhood. Unle Eli and I would go out around two,
walking hand in hand through the portals that led to the cafe
and wouldn't come back to the store until after three, both of
us laughing and giggling, while I held a big coconut ice cream
cone in my hand. My father started to get suspicious of our
long daily escapades and one day followed us to the cafe and
hid behind a column, next to a huge mahogany breakfront
where pastries were displayed, and the growing number of
customers that kept coming in couldn't see him. He waited
there for a while and then, intrigued by the crowd, worked his
way in to the first row and to his amazement discovered the
object of every one's attention: There I was, on top of one of
the marble-topped tables and next to a picture of the Buddha,
a mini-replica of Carmen Miranda, shimmying and shaking to
the tune of the latest rumba. Uncle Eli was in the middle of a
big circle, under a ceiling fan, clapping and laughing at the
impromptu show. "That's my niece! That's my niece," he was
screaming at the top of his lungs when my father caught up

with him. Needless to say that was my last dancing escapade. Uncle Eli and I were barred from going together again to the *Cafe de los Chinos*, not even for ice cream, a chore that my father undertook from then on.

It follows that my grandfather Maximo was the serious brother. He had an inquiring mind and managed to maintain a degree of Jewish intellectuality even in our remote little island. The high point of his week was the arrival of the *Forward*. The minute the Jewish newspaper arrived in the store, his eyes would light up and that was my signal to follow him to the back where there was a small dining room and a kitchen. It was there, in front of a strong cup of tea, that he would read out loud story after story in Yiddish, which he would later translate for me into Spanish. That's how I first learned about Jews in other parts of the world, about the old life in Europe and about the struggle to establish a Jewish state. The *Forward* arrived every week from New York and every week it opened for us a new window to the richness of Jewish life. I realize now how alienated from his roots Grandfather must have felt, and how much he longed for the warmth of the tiny Jewish *shtetl* where he had grown up.

His response, like that of many other Jews in Cuba was to surround himself with a group of friends that shared his experiences and reminded him of home. Consequently there were many card games at the Cerro apartment, where my grandfather would sit in a rocking chair and entertain his guests playing the mandolin. This instrument, which he had brought from Lithuania, fascinated me and he would sometimes, to my delight, let me play a few notes on the small guitar.

When my mother was young, way before I was born, she

accompanied my grandfather at the piano while all the family listened: uncle Eli, my aunt Pessl, my uncle Jaime, her cousins Lilia and Rafaela as well as their card-playing friends; among them a young man called Sam Lewin who lived with my grandparents for a while. Sam and my grandfather used to sell ties in the streets when they first came to Cuba. They would take turns tying a big wooden box with a strap around the neck and walk around announcing their wares until they would get to a propitious corner, lay it down on the floor and start taking care of customers. That memory of the early days held them together for many years, even way after prosperity set in and Sam would come often to the Cerro apartment where Yiddish songs would fill the air with the music of the mandolin and the piano, and a slice of Europe would shine right under the tropical sky.

This tight social circle extended to young people as well, since all social interchange was confined to sons and daughters of friends and of people within the community, a fact that restricted my mother's social life. As a young girl she had been an ugly duckling. Early pictures show delicate features and big blue eyes which were dwarfed by a nose that just sat there in the middle of an otherwise beautiful face. To top if off, her cousins were pretty girls, and even her brother was a handsome rambunctious little boy. As she grew up she compensated with a good figure and a sweet, gregarious personality, but the unfairness of her looks took a toll on her self-esteem. My grandmother worshipped physical beauty and whenever a pretty girl would walk into the store she would rave about her attributes until even I felt pretty uncomfortable, not to mention how my mother must have felt in view of her shortcoming. She had the classical Jewish hook nose and no matter how much she pleaded with my grand-

31

parents and later on with my father, to let her travel to the States and have it fixed, she had to live with that insult way into her later years when, after my father's death, I took her to the best plastic surgeon in Miami who gave her not only a new nose, but a new life and towards the end she was considered by everyone who met her a truly beautiful woman— something that gave her —and me— an inordinate amount of pleasure.

But be it as it may, from the moment I was born I used to hear that when she was pregnant she would look at pictures of beautiful girls and visualize the most beautiful nose so that I would be born with one. "How lucky you are that you don't look like me!" she would exclaim staring proudly at the tiny button nose I was born with. "Thank God you look like your father!"

I wanted to *be* like my father! A good-looking man with blonde hair, golden skin and chiseled features, he had an innate *joie-de-vivre*, and adapted to the Cuban way of life like fish take to water. His business put him in touch with many people, Jews as well as non-Jews and he made strong, lasting friendships with many of the Spaniards that dominated the Cuban commercial establishment with whom he conducted business. In their social circle he was the star, and my mother the supporting actress. He had an irreverence towards life that cut through the very soul of the Cuban people, who loved his ability to laugh everything off.

Nobody knew then that his irreverence came from a deeper well, a well full of memories that even then I had the feeling he'd rather leave alone. It wasn't anything that I could put my finger on, but whenever a conversation started about Europe or the good old days in the old country, he became impatient and changed the subject. "We're here," he'd say, isn't that enough?

If life would have been so wonderful there, we would have never come to Cuba!" he used to retort to my grandfather's frequent allusions to his beloved *Lita*, which he had left way before the horrors of the war started. On those occasions my mother would stick her face into a book or simply walk out on the excuse of having something to do. She tried to avoid at all costs getting my father upset, and so did I, since once provoked, he had a truly awful temper.

All my mother seemed to crave was peace and quiet. "Don't you get bored staying home all day?" I often asked her. "That's what women are supposed to do," was her simple answer, as she proceeded to pour out homemade pudding into pretty parfait cups so they would have time to gel and be perfectly cold before my father came home. She had wanted to work with her husband like so many of her friends did, but my father would not hear of it. He wanted her home with the children and she, like so many women of her generation, turned all her energies into raising my brother and I, channeling all her dreams and hopes into the two of us. She had a good head for business and a discriminating taste for music and art, but my father's strong personality obliterated her feeble attempts at asserting herself, preferring instead to play second fiddle to his sparkling, jovial nature and he compensated by using his considerable charm to bring laughter and sunshine into her mellow, subdued universe.

My father's distinctive whistle always let us know when he was home. We would start hearing it as he came up the stairs and, as soon as he opened the door, a thin veil of gray would lift all around us as sunshine followed his steps. He would fondle my mother when he thought I was not looking, plant a big kiss on my cheek and tell a funny story that would invariably be followed by his contagious laughter. A few minutes later he would start an argument over nothing and we knew that life, as we knew it, was on once again.

Soon after moving in with my grandparents I started kindergarten and for the first time I could play with children my own age. The school was right across the street from my father's store, and after class my mother or the maid would pick me up and I would wait at the store, peering through the glass cases that held belts and custom jewelry and looking out for Milagros, a little black girl that became my best friend. Every day after class Milagros would come and play house with me. We would sit on the floor, among bolts of fabric and shoe boxes and start fashioning sofas and chairs for our imaginary house by stacking up soap bars that my father sold in the store. I was fascinated by her tight coarse braids and she would let me untie them and run my fingers through her hair. I in turn would let her run a comb through my blonde soft tresses. "Your hair is so shiny!" she would exclaim, and I would run and get a pot of Vaseline to put on hers. Other days we would walk up to my grandparents apartment, which they built on the top floor of a building they owned near the store. There on the rooftop my grandfather Maximo built a gazebo where he hung two green canvas hammocks and Milagros and I would each climb into a hammock and laze the afternoon away, watching the birds feed on the bread crumbs Grandfather would scatter for them every morning before leaving for work. Rocking myself in the hammock I would stare at the blue sky and imagine myself far, far away, beyond the white soft clouds the birds would escape to after their daily feast.

AZABACHES AND AVE MARIAS

My dreamy, placid life would turn around Christmas and it would not go back to normal until after Three Kings Day. I was mesmerized by the activity that went on all around me, and loved the pageantry and color that the season brought, but it only served to point out how different I was from most everyone I knew. Christmas time the Calzada del Cerro became one big fairyland, where vendors displayed all kinds of wonderful toys under the big portals that lined the streets. There were stuffed animals and moving mechanical dogs, beautiful dolls encased in cellophane-wrapped boxes, with white and black faces, colorful Christmas decorations and big Christmas trees. I couldn't walk from my grandfather's house to the store without walking by this yearly wonderland. To top it all the family of the boy next door used to put up the biggest Christmas tree of anyone in the neighborhood and I was always called in to help decorate it. The whole family would gather to open the boxes full of shiny balls and tinsel and we would take turns going up a ladder to put up the colorful Christmas balls in the branches of the huge tree. It was too much to bear for a little girl, I wanted my own tree!

One year I cried so much that my mother went out and bought me a small tree, which my father took no time in taking apart as soon as he came home. "Jews don't put up Christmas trees in their homes!" he yelled as he bent each branch in half and scattered the beautiful balls and ribbons of tinsel on the floor. I ran out and hid in my room for the rest of the evening, my heart broken together with the shattered shiny Christmas balls. Eventually we made a bargain. We would overlook Christmas and I would get my presents on Three Kings Day. *El Día de los Reyes* (Three Kings Day) was the day when the

Magi arrived at the home of Joseph and Mary bearing gifts for Jesus and the one day of the year when all children in Cuba, even the poorest of the poor, would get at least one toy.

After the incident with the Christmas tree, my grandparents decided that it was time for me to enroll in the Jewish school and we rented an apartment in Old Havana, where the Centro Israelita, the Jewish center which housed the school, occupied an old turn-of-the-century mansion on Egido Street.

I did not want to move, but had not much to say on the matter since the decision had been taken, and we worked for days putting all our belongings away in big boxes in preparation for the move. Everybody in the store helped out and my grandmother, my mother and the maid got busy tidying things up around the apartment and making sure we had not forgotten anything. Even my toys had been put away and I was sitting waiting for the movers and feeling pretty low when Milagros walked in with her mother to say good-bye.

As soon as I saw her I ran to her. I wanted to take her by the hand, go back to my grandfather's apartment and jump on a hammock, but stopped when I realized that she was hiding something behind her back. She walked slowly and carefully, avoiding my eyes and trying not to let me see what she was hiding. Finally when she was only a few steps away, she stood solemnly in front of me and, her shining black eyes brimming with tears, handed me her parting present: a small black doll. The face of the doll, like the rest of her body, was made of cotton fabric and her black braids were fashioned out of yarn and held together by two red ribbons. "This is for you," she said, running away, "So you won't forget me."

I ran after her, but she was faster than me and by the time I got to the corner I saw her turn into the street where she lived. I looked back. Nobody was following me. With the commotion of the move they had not noticed that I had run out. I kept on walking and saw Milagros disappear into a *solar*, one of the one-room apartment buildings where many of the blacks lived, which had been carved out of big colonial houses, partitioned and rented out to low-income families. I walked under a line hung with freshly-washed clothes and the smell of soap and lye filled my nostrils as I avoided a tin container laid out to catch the approaching rain. I knew where Milagros lived, for we had dropped her home one day in front of the building, and I went up one flight of steps to a big open hallway flanked on both sides by green doors. Each room had a wooden door and one window with iron grates as its only ventilation and source of light, and each window faced the interior balcony, where some of the tenants grew small plants in pots and pans. A cat was drinking milk out of a small bowl in front of one of the doors. It was her cat. I knocked and Milagros' mother answered.

"She's not here," she said, peering from behind the door. "She's probably hiding downstairs at one of the neighbors."

"But why," I asked, "Why did she run away from me?"

Milagros' mother opened the door just a crack, without asking me to come in. "It may be hard for you to understand what I'm going to tell you, but one day you will," she said, and then, adjusting the band of her house dress and placing her hands squarely on her hips, looked at me straight in the eyes : "You see, Milagros will never leave the *solar*. Her life, like mine and my mother's before me has been mapped out for her. She will grow up, marry, have children and live out her life right here where she was born among the lines of clothes, the prowling cats and the screaming children. In the summer she will stand the heat in these four walls without ventilation like I do and at night she will listen to every neighbor's snores and coughs before waking up early to go to work. You belong to a different world. Anything is possible for you. This is your first move, but it won't be your last. Milagros will never meet anyone like you, you mean everything to her, but your lives are too different. Better you part now so each of you can go your own way. *Vamos*," she said and started walking in front of me, her wooden sandals clip-clopping down the stairs. I followed her silently, while curtains raised in our wake as curious neighbors looked out, and as I followed her down the metal stairs I saw a pair of small black eyes peering from behind one of the doors. I waved good-bye and turned my face quickly, so that Milagros couldn't see the tears that were now rolling down my own cheeks.

Milagros' mother turned out to be right. I never saw my little friend again. Old Havana beckoned far away from El Cerro. Life was richer here, and mine took a very different turn. Old Havana was the hub of the Jewish community at the time, where most of the fabric stores and small shoe and textile manufacturers were located, and my father opened a small lingerie *atelier* in nearby Villegas Street. Our apartment had very high ceilings, which allowed the cooling breezes to circulate in the summer, and a wrought-iron balcony became a front-row seat to the teeming life of the city in all its splendor. Lottery vendors chanted the numbers while they carried the full *billetes* high in the air, tempting the buyers with instant riches. Every once in a while I would hear a singsong: *"Tengo mango, mango del Caney,* *mamey colorad*o." These were the pregones, melodious chants the fruit vendors would intone in order to entice the housewives to come down and sample their delicious fruit. *"Tengo mango, mango del Caney"*, they would chant, referring to the sweet big mangoes from Oriente province, their succulent meat orangey yellow and juicy, "mamey colorado", the red, custard-like meaty fruit that grows only in the full summer or the white pineapple, the queen of the tropical fruits. Not to mention the anones and zapotes, each one more enticing than the other. We would chill the fruit in the ice box and feast on them in the hot summer months. "Forget food, just give me the fruits of summer", my father would say as he came home exhausted after a scorching day in the cutting room. (This was before the days of air conditioning). Luckily the high ceilings and the fan alleviated the heat, but we still suffered the effects of the hot Cuban summers— probably the only thing my father did not appreciate about his beloved island, since he couldn't stay too long in the sun without blistering. It wasn't until summer's end, after months of spending weekends at the beach spreading all kinds of oils on his fair skin that he would acquire a golden tan which would then last for most of the year. The beach was our playground, our birth right and our sanctuary and everyone in Cuba, from the poorest to the richest, had their own spot in the sun.

As soon as we moved back to Havana, I was surrounded by a full entourage of cousins, aunts and uncles. My mother's two unmarried cousins, Lilia and Rafaela, came to the house often. They were attractive and feminine young women who were up on the latest trends and I enjoyed spending time around them. Lilia's long nails were manicured weekly by a lady that came to our apartment. As soon as Hortensia came in, the maid would make a fresh pot of strong, sweet coffee which she served in tiny cups. After getting up-to-date on the latest gossip, we would then all sit around the dining room table watching the manicurist pull out all sort of small bottles from a black bag, where she also kept small scissors and cotton balls. She would then spread everything on the table on top of a small towel, whereupon she would begin applying a dark red, pearlized polish on Lilia's nails, carefully drawing a white half moon at the base. I would sit and watch, fascinated by the colors and the designs that Hortenisa would create on each one of Lilia's nails and every once in a while I would sneak in a touch of polish on one of my own short nails that I had to hide from my father, so he wouldn't make me take it off.

Since Cuba is an island, the only way to leave is by boat or plane, a fact that has often worked politically against it. But back in the 40's taking an airplane and leaving the country was a big undertaking that carried undertones of adventure and therefore, a whole family event. When Rafaela, my mother's younger cousin, got married and emigrated to Philadelphia, we all dressed in our Sunday best and went to Rancho Boyeros Airport to bid her and her new husband farewell. They were emigrating to "El Norte", where they would start a whole new life away from our close-knit family group. My grandmother and my aunt Pessl baked cookies for them to eat on the plane and we all stood behind a glass wall watching the motors begin to spin, waving frantically when the big Pan American Clipper took off like a huge silver bird, and didn't stop waving until we saw its diminishing outline disappear into the blue, cloud-dotted sky.

"We have to write to her as soon as we get home," said uncle Jaime once we were all seated in the car for the ride back to Havana.

"Jaime, we don't even have an address yet. Let them first find an apartment," said Pessl, bringing one hand to her chest while she used the other to blow her nose with a lace-trimmed handkerchief she often used during her performances in the Yiddish theater. She was a tall, beautiful woman with an imposing presence and my uncle endured philosophically her frequent appearances at the *Dramatishe Sektzie.*

One of the amateur actresses that appeared with my aunt Pessl in the Yiddish theater was a young woman named Sasha. She was known just by her first name. It was really a man's name but that's how everybody knew her, just Sasha. It was enough. Sasha was without a doubt the most beautiful Jewish girl in all Havana. She had creamy ivory skin, almond-shaped black eyes that glistened like a pair of glass marbles and curly black hair that she wore in a bob, which ended up making her look almost Oriental.

Sasha was the star of every show and every man that saw her carried a secret crush on her. Sasha enjoyed her life, which is to say she did exactly as she pleased. She had come to Cuba without her parents and was too young to be spoken for — and far too smart to allow it at her age. Consequently she had a retinue of boyfriends that were always ready to entertain her as lavishly as it was possible in those days. Tongues wagged, and Sasha kept on acting and enjoying her freedom, riding on motorcycles with the rest of her acting, bohemian band of friends feeling as happy as any woman had a right to feel in the Havana of the 1930's.

THE LAST MINYAN IN HAVANA

One night a young, tall man with bad skin was sitting in the audience when Sasha appeared in one of Sholem Aleijem's plays. He sat in the back, entranced by Sasha's performance. The way she held her handkerchief in her delicate fingers, the way she turned her shoulder on her abusive husband, reduced Sam Lewin to tears. He waited for her outside the theater at the end of the performance and introduced himself, offering to walk her home. After that day Sam wouldn't leave Sasha's side and after a while, one by one, she stopped seeing her other boyfriends. It wasn't that Sam was so enchanting. He wasn't. Or so rich. He could barely take care of himself. He was just there. Not only when her performance was great, but also when she had an off day. Not only when she was her usual, cheerful self, but also when she was feeling low or cranky. And when one day Sam brought Sasha to my grandparent's home for lunch they did not have the heart to tell him about Sasha's past, since obviously he was totally besotted with her.

So Sam married Sasha and continued his career as a traveling salesman. Soon after, Sasha gave birth to a little girl, whom she named Rina. I used to go to Rina's birthdays and she used to come to mine, but we did not become good friends until many years later. Eventually Sasha grew restless of staying home and, being now a married woman, diverted her considerable energy into starting a business of her own, manufacturing costume jewelry. She would wait until Rina left for school and, sitting at the kitchen table, would start fashioning earrings out of buttons and tiny shells which she embellished with all sort of colorful sprinkles. She started selling her small production to people like my grandfather who ran small general stores and eventually hired some helpers, until she accumu-

42

lated enough orders to build a small factory, which eventually grew into a big one. Her brand became synonymous with a certain kind of jewelry that evoked the feeling of the tropics and she started to export, primarily to the United States. Sasha Lewin became the first woman industrialist in Havana — and an inspiration to a whole generation of women who refused to fit the old mold.

On my father's side I had two uncles and an aunt. My uncle Jacobo, the oldest, had been the first to emigrate from Poland and saved enough money to bring my father, my aunt Eugenia and my uncle Fernando, the youngest of the boys. Four more sisters stayed behind and I never heard much about them, only that they were killed in the Holocaust. My father fended any questions about that subject, so I learned to curb my natural curiosity and to concentrate instead on the family at hand. I was closest to my aunt Gitel, who changed her name to Eugenia in Cuba, and lived in another province. Eugenia had two sons, Pepe and Jaime. Jaime, the youngest, was three years older than me. Blonde and mischievous, with a constant twinkle in his eye, he became my hero. We had a picture of him standing in front of the gate of his country house and I would look at it and dream of the summers when I would go to Matanzas to stay with them for weeks at a time.

The Cuban countryside is lush, with verdant fields that extend over tranquil valleys dotted with stately royal palms and *bohios*, the thatched-roofed humble houses of the *campesinos* that are covered with dried palm fronds. The rich, red soil yields generous crops of sugar, coffee, bananas and a variety of vegetables and tropical fruits that grow abundantly in the fertile plains where water and sunshine are plentiful all year round. The western province of Pinar del Rio is home to the tobacco industry. It is there, in the region known as Vuelta Abajo, where soil, water and sunshine have converged to create the one place in the world were the best tobacco leaf can grow. Nowhere else on earth do these propitious conditions exist and the big, jade-green tobacco leaves stretch over acres of red soil only interrupted here and there by the A-shaped timber barns where they are hung to dry. Pinar del Rio is also home to the beautiful valley of Viñales that is surrounded by *mogotes*, spectacular prehistoric formations shaped like an inverted U that lend this valley its unique topography, created over millions of years through erosion of the softer earth around them.

Matanzas province, where my cousin lived, is better known by Varadero, a powdery-sand beach with turquoise waters that rivals some of the best in the world and stretches for several miles over the Northern Atlantic coast.

Built on the Hicacos Peninsula, a rocky sliver of land edged with soft white sand and ringed by a coral reef, the resort town of Varadero faces West to the Atlantic just over 120 miles South of Key West. It was the proximity to Florida that attracted the attention of American industrialist Ireene Dupont, who built a palatial summer home in the very tip of the peninsula back in the 1920's. Always the businessman, Dupont also purchased additional land, which he then sold to his many friends. Over the next few decades, more Americans moved into the area in the summer, renting the fine old beach houses that had been built on that land, and also building their own.

AZABACHES AND AVE MARIAS

Over the years the Dupont enclave remained a secluded beach resort for foreigners. There were rumors about rum-running during the Prohibition, of wild parties thrown by Dupont in the forties and of movie stars like Esther Williams, Cary Grant and Ava Gardner sunning themselves by the beach in the fifties. But Varadero was always popular with the local people and we spent many glorious holidays at the Kawama Hotel, sleeping in bungalows right on the sand and feasting on paella cooked with seafood that had been swimming in the ocean just a few hours before. During the *corrida del camarón*, the time of the year at the end of winter when shrimp run in the many waterways that surround the peninsula, people would just put their buckets out and come home with hundreds of shrimp ready to be cooked in the most delicious dishes.

I knew I was in Banaguises, the small Matanzas town where my cousin lived, as soon as I smelled the musty odor of the fresh, red, soil and saw the *colonos*, their feet encased in tall rust leather boots riding their shiny horses. My uncle waited for us at the train station and after many hugs and kisses, would take me and my mother to their country store, which had a big wooden house in the back. The store was airy and open and sold everything that the farmers and land-owners needed, from work clothes to boots, belts and hats. The house, that connected in the back, wrapped around a colonial patio where flowering plants grew in clay pots and planters —bright red geraniums, fragrant gardenias and the coveted *mariposa*, a delicate white flower, shaped like a butterfly that is indigenous to the island.

By the time we got to the store my aunt Eugenia was invariably waiting outside for us. "There you are! Look how much she's grown! Come here, let me take a good look at you," she'd say, turning me around, her dark-blonde braids neatly arranged in a bun at her nape. "Paulina, she's going to be tall, but she's too skinny. Asuncion is preparing a delicious *potaje de garbanzos*, she'll love it!" she'd say and she would disappear through the curtain that led to the house to supervise lunch.

Being in Banaguises was for me a wonderful retreat. The calm of the countryside contrasted sharply with the lively commotion of Havana and I enjoyed reading from my cousins' vast book collection. My favorites were the tales of Hans Christian Andersen that I would read and reread, learning all about dragons, castles and princesses. There I was also exposed for the first time to classical music. My aunt had a beautiful voice and on ocassions when my mother and I visited, she would play classical pieces in an old record player and sing arias from famous operas while we sat entranced in their big airy living room that a ceiling fan kept comfortable in the summer, surrounded by pictures of sullen-faced relatives I had never met.

On weekends we would sometimes visit the *Central Rosario*, the sugar mill close to Banaguises. There, acres of sugarcane, the lifeblood of the town, were harvested every year at the time of the *zafra*, when every able-bodied man would wield his *machete* to cut down the sweet, proud stalks that would be processed into *guarapo* (sugar cane juice) and later distilled into crystallized sugar, mountains of which sparkled like diamonds every *zafra* in the back of the *Central* under the bright Cuban sun.

Other times I would go with my cousin and the maid in long excursions to the nearby countryside, where we would pick mangoes from the trees and sit and eat them under the shade of the tree, the Cuban way. We would prick the skin with our teeth and suck the juicy pulp through the opening, the juice dripping through our fingers, until, our bellies full and our mouths yellow and sticky, we would walk back contentedly to the big wooden house behind the store, where we would get a bath and a light reprimand with the promise of a sure indigestion.

In the evening, as the town began to darken and cool off after the hot day, we would go to the movie house, set in a big hall, where everyone would bring their own chair and watch Mexican tear jerkers starring Jorge Negrete, Latin America's matinee idol at that time. Later I would fall asleep to the hum of a ceiling fan, in a bed covered by a mosquito net and wait for a new day.

Uncle Eli.

Standing: Lilia and my mother.
Seated: Rafaela and uncle Moshe, shortly
after arriving in Havana, 1927.

Typical stained-glass windows in Old Havana.

My aunt Eugenia in
Matanzas, 1946.

Right: Afro-Cuban show in
today's Tropicana.

Below: The Parque Central
with the Capitolio in the
background.

My mother and father (foreground)
at a celebration in Havana, 1945.

My mother and father in Aguacate, 1940.

The author at the age of three.

My father with my baby brother, 1949.

Parque de la Fraternidad with the old ceiba tree.

Stained glass window in a chocolate shop in today's Havana.

The statue of Jose Marti dominates the Parque Central.

2

EL CABALLERO DE PARIS
AND OTHER CHARACTERS

One bright September morning my mother and I left our Old Havana apartment and walked to Egido Street for my first day of school. On the way the streets started opening up, from the narrow and crowded grid that prevailed inside the city core, to the pleasant symmetry of the boulevards that adjoined the Parque Central. I was nervous and held her hand tightly, but at the same time enjoyed the novelty of it all. The big colonial buildings, the bright sunshine that highlighted the intense color of the flowers laid out in perfect rows around the park, with the shining dome of the Capitolio in the back, the slight change in the breeze, all contributed to the mounting excitement. It was a beautiful part of the city and we had never walked this way before.

When we got to the corner of Egido Street she held me closely, for we had to cross a wide avenue and traffic was starting to get heavy, so we stopped in front of a cart full of oranges while we waited for traffic to subside. My mother selected an orange and the Chinese vendor peeled it in a rotary peeler and handed it to her smooth and juicy, ready to eat. We bought a bag for home and she had him cut one in half and wrap it for me to eat at recess. The exhaust fumes of the cars mingled with the smell of the flowers and the tangy aroma of the oranges as we crossed the busy avenue. In front of us a big two-story gray building stood in a corner, adorned on each side with graceful balconies that reached out to the busy street below. We entered the portal that led to the school and went up the big marble staircase of the Centro Israelita, my hand following the smooth, cool black wrought-iron railing that curved gracefully all the way up to the second floor.

The headquarters of the Jewish community, where the school was located, had been an old mansion in its heyday, what was called in Havana a *palacete* or small palace, which had been inhabited at the turn of the century by an upper-class family, but the city grew to the outskirts and the neighborhood that had once been grand had now lost its former glory. The building, however, had retained all of its old charm, with its many rooms, now converted into classrooms, extending around a U-shaped inner balcony that overlooked a spacious courtyard planted with all sorts of greenery, and after the first awkward moments, I settled easily into the school routine, learning the letters and words I had half-guessed months before.

My one trouble spot was Yiddish. In those days we had to memorize long history lessons in a foreign language without ever being explained the meaning of the words. The teacher's assumption was that my parents, like most did, spoke it at home. But my father preferred to speak to me in Spanish, and that task was taken over by my uncle Moises, my aunt Eugenia's husband, who had studied at a *yeshiva* and relished the experience of teaching a little girl about *Yiddishe Geshichte* whenever he was in Havana, where he came often on shopping trips to stock his country store. Needless to say, Yiddish was my worst subject in school, since half the time I had to memorize long lessons that I repeated like a parrot, without knowing the meaning of what I was saying and using a different alphabet. My mother wasn't much help either, since her knowledge of Yiddish was also limited, so I accepted my fate and lived in dread of the afternoon session, which was conducted entirely in that language.

One day, while I was trying to memorize a particularly difficult lesson, I heard someone coming up the stairs. I ran out to the hallway and saw my mother, her legs covered in blood, struggling up the narrow, dark staircase that led to our apartment. I screamed for the maid and between the two of us helped her inside and cleaned her up. She was in the early stages of pregnancy and had stumbled and fallen in the street. My father came running from the store and called the doctor, who confirmed that she had miscarried, and prescribed bed rest. For a whole week after that incident my father would come home and go directly to the bedroom to check on my mother's condition. No jokes and no funny stories. He would sit on the bed, next to the mahogany dresser with a half-moon mirror in front of which my mother would brush her dark wavy hair in the mornings, and stay in for a long time, making sure she was resting in the proper position, that her legs were elevated and that she had everything she needed. When he would finally come out his eyes were invariably red and, whenever he thought I was not looking, he would take out an old photograph from his shirt pocket and stare at it longingly. Somehow I knew that picture did not belong to any of us, but I did not dare ask whose it was. All I knew was that it was upsetting my father and was part of that uncharted territory that belonged to another world, a world I could only guess at by the stories my grandfather and my aunt sometimes shared with me but they, too, left a lot of questions unanswered and soon that alien place started to acquire an ominous nature and I started to believe, like my father, that it was better left alone.

A few months later I noticed that my mother was getting big again. This time she looked completely happy and content, so I gathered that something wonderful was going to happen. They finally told me that she was going to have a baby. To avoid another miscarriage, my father insisted that she didn't leave the apartment until the baby was born — even our groceries were delivered. But my mother didn't seem to mind her confinement. Pregnancy was her most exalted time and once again she prayed for a beautiful baby.

As it happens, she had a vision after her miscarriage. She had been sitting up in bed at night, fanning herself with a big sandalwood fan, like she often did when she couldn't sleep, the sweet smell of the wood lulling her senses, when she saw a white handkerchief dance before her eyes. Suddenly it stopped and landed softly on her head. "That moment a feeling of total peace surrounded me and I knew that I was going to get pregnant again and that I was going to have a baby boy," she told me years later over a cup of tea, in the course of an afternoon when we were exchanging confidences, her face beaming anew with the recollection.

From the moment she found out she was pregnant, my mother sat for hours at a time next to a tall window in our living room embroidering the baby's trousseau. There were blankets adorned by playful angels and hemmed in by delicate lace and I sat by her side, watching the sunlight illuminate the round hoop that stretched the material so she could apply the colorful stitches, one by one. Clouds, harps and music notes would eventually emerge from under her nimble fingers as the months went by and her belly grew bigger and bigger.

My brother Michael was auspiciously born the same week that Israel gained independence. When my mother and the new baby came home from the hospital, the whole family was at the apartment listening to the tally of the votes from the countries that formed the United Nations. The results were coming to us haltingly from a big wooden radio we had in the living room. Uncle Eli kept turning the knobs to get a better reception, but the rumble of the static kept getting in the way of the announcements that were being broadcast by the Cuban radio station. Finally Cuba's vote came in and we strained to listen. To our surprise, the Cuban delegate voted against the establishment of a Jewish state, making Cuba the only Latin American country that voted against the partition of Palestine. President Grau San Martin and his delegate, Guillermo Belt, considered a vote pro Israel a politically incorrect move vis-a-vis Cuba's relations with the Arab states.

The rest of the broadcast was difficult to understand. There were still ten countries that needed to cast their votes. We waited next to the radio the rest of the afternoon until finally my father became impatient and asked me to go out with him to get a newspaper. We walked for a couple of blocks through the narrow cobblestone streets where the neighborhood women stood outside open doors, talking and fanning themselves in the purple light of early evening. I tried to avoid the cats that meandered through the narrow sidewalks while I held on to my father's hand until, about four blocks from our apartment, we finally found a newspaper stand next to a corner cafe. My father paid the attendant and stood under a street light concentrating on the story that appeared under the bold headlines.

"Papi, tell me what it says," I finally asked impatiently. I could make out some of the letters from the tall headlines, but others escaped me.

"We have our own country, and it's called Israel," he said, waving the newspaper in front of my startled eyes. In spite of Cuba's opposition, the vote for the partition had come through! We rushed back to share the news of the new Jewish state with my grandparents and my uncle Eli; my grandmother came out of the kitchen carrying a dish of eggs with *gribenes* —my father's favorite— and we celebrated the two births.

Suddenly my brother started to cry. He needed a change and I ran in to watch what they were doing. I was standing next to him fascinated by what I found under the diaper when that little thing sprung to life and he ended up peeing all over me.

"Mazel tov!" cried out uncle Eli as he doubled up in laughter.

"Kein an hora!" said Grandma Sara, who took every opportunity to find a lucky omen, and I ran away to get out of my wet clothes.

As it happens, a page in the early history of Israel was written with Cuban blood. Shortly after the establishment of the State of Israel a group of seven Cuban college students from the

Macabi movement decided to leave the comfort of their Havana homes in order to join the Israeli forces in their fight against the Arabs. From Havana they flew to the port of Marseilles where they boarded the Altalena, a ship that was to transport armaments to Tel Aviv. But way before the Altalena had a chance to reach Israeli shores the two titans that controlled the destiny of the new nation had come to a showdown. Menachem Begin espoused the hard line of the Irgun in his dealings with the Arab enemies that already haunted the new nation, while David Ben Gurion preferred a policy of reason and diplomacy.

Oblivious to the quirks of history, the young fighters boarded the Altalena in the middle of June and spent two days hauling ammunition. The war in Europe had ended just a few years before and displaced persons where being shifted all over the continent. Consequently the Altalena was also being used to smuggle Jews into Israel, taking close to a thousand refugees from all parts of Europe on their way to the promised land. The defense group came to close to sixty, with volunteers from England and the U.S. joining the Cuban boys. After two days in Marseilles they sailed through the Mediterranean sea en route to Tel Aviv, having to avoid several British ships on the way, for fear that their human cargo would cause a detour to Cyprus, where new refugees en route to Israel were still being detained. The refugees were left off at Kfar Vitkin, a coastal town half an hour away from Tel Aviv. There Menachem Begin came on board to greet the volunteers and left quietly before the ship's arrival into the port city.

But a reception of the wrong kind awaited the Altalena. About 300 meters from the coast of Tel Aviv the ship started getting shot at by sharp shooters from the Haganah who were positioned on the rooftops of the nearby city buildings. Unbeknown to the volunteers, Begin had requested the arms that were being carried in the Altalena for the militant Irgun and Ben Gurion refused, giving orders to shoot at the Altalena in order to avoid the arms and ammunition from coming ashore.

One of the bullets hit Daniel Levy, a first year medical student from Havana on the forehead, killing him on the spot. Another wounded David Mitrani, a law student, mortally. The barrage of bullets hit the ship's storage room, which was full of ammunition, and a minute later it was up in flames. The captain promptly ordered the ship flooded in order to avoid an explosion. The rest of the crew and passengers jumped overboard and started to swim to shore. In total thirteen people died in the Altalena in plain view of Tel Aviv. The surviving volunteers joined the Irgun, which shortly after made peace with the Haganah and, together with the Palmaj came to form what is known today as the Israeli Defense Forces.

The names of Levy and Mitrani can be seen in a stone monument erected by the sea in Tel Aviv, in the same spot where the Altalena went up in flames. A sea many miles away from the one these boys knew, in a country they cared enough about to lose their young lives and sacrifice their unrealized dreams for.

From the moment my brother was born my life underwent a drastic change. During the first year of his life my mother was not allowed to leave him alone. My father simply would not trust anybody else to care for the baby. As overprotective as he had been of me, he became even more so of that new baby boy. He had wanted a boy so badly! He would stand next to his crib and carry long conversations with him as the baby kicked his legs and tried to focus his still myopic eyes on my father. "We're finally going to have a doctor in the family," he'd say, declaring my brother's profession from the very day he was born, his own dream of becoming a doctor, prematurely extinguished years before in Poland, now hopefully reborn with his first son. This tiny baby was going to go to medical school and he was going to be addressed by everyone as "Dr. Tuchman." And he, Haim, would sit and discuss medical lessons with him when he came home from the university; meet his professors, encourage him to become the best doctor in Havana and yes he, Haim, was going to be, believe or not, the doctor's father! My father's happiness knew no limits, and neither did his plans for his new baby boy.

I, on the other hand, felt suddenly abandoned. My father's new edict prevented my mother from going out with me and I had to go with the maid or with my grandmother or a neighbor to places where she would have usually taken me before. Eventually I became used to my sudden abandonment and took it philosophically, which is to say I went on with my usual routine, without my mother. After the school afternoon session was over, the maid would pick me up carrying a pair of skates and off we would go to the Parque de la Fraternidad, where a huge ceiba tree, said to be two hundred years old, was encased in a circular black iron fence. There I would put on my skates and skate around the tree for hours while the maid sat on one of the old-fashioned wooden benches and gossiped with her friends. Later on friends would join me and we would do fancy skating under the shade of the big tree. Some of Havana's characters would congregate at the park to add color to our sunny afternoons.

My favorite was el *Caballero de Paris* (the Knight from Paris), a madman who wore a black cape and long hair and walked around the park selling colorful carved pens, his sandaled feet expertly navigating the cracks that the gnarled tree roots would cause in the cement. Every once in a while someone would buy a pen and el *Caballero* would take one out of a black canvas bag he always carried with him, attach to it a colored feather with a flourish and regale his customer with a story from his days of youth when he claimed to have roamed the world. I only watched him from a distance, afraid of his getup, but fascinated by him all the same. At four o'clock the vendor with the flavored ices would show up and all the kids would stop skating to run to his cart for a *duro frío* that we would lick in the hot summer afternoon standing in the grass so as not to fall with our skates (this was before they put brakes on skates).

The Parque de la Fraternidad was across the street from the Capitolio and the Parque Central, the civic center of Old Havana, and the most beautiful part of the city. With its wide boulevards, green areas and flower beds, it echoed the parks of the grand cities of Europe, only in a much smaller scale. The Capitolio was a copy of the one in Washington, D.C. and two monumental bronze statues flanked both sides of the wide stairs. A huge diamond was encased, very much like the one in Istanbul's Palace of Topkapi, on top of the Capitolio Dome, and in spite of its constant surveillance, it disappeared one day. Years later it was rumored that it had ended in the pocket of one of Cuba's corrupt presidents, a fact that did not surprise anyone.

One of my fondest memories was of watching the Comparsas with my parents during Carnival time. Comparsas were the regional dance groups of the blacks and they would come down the Parque Central during Lent, dressed in colorful costumes, *arrollando* through the boulevards of Havana following the bands. On that special Saturday night my parents took me to a restaurant that had streetside tables with a view of the procession. There, under one of the big portals that line the avenues of Havana, we sat at a table covered with a white crisp tablecloth and watched the costumed dancers while we dined, as wave after wave of them danced their way down the Parque Central, their bodies moving sinuously to the rhythm of ancestral Afro-Cuban sounds. Dancers and spectators caught the fever alike, moving as if in a trance, the street lights and neon signs lending a festive air in the distance while the old *bongo* players hit the stretched leather of their instruments time and again with their black fingers and the side of their outstretched palms, their spirit transcending their music, a big flash of white teeth illuminating their black ecstatic faces.

It was a magical sight for a seven-year-old. The monuments, the dancers, the beautifully coifed and dressed men and women who sat next to us watching the show. Only once, on my first visit to Paris was I touched by some of the same magic, but, alas, there was no music and no dancing in the streets!

Before embarking on their tragic mission: David Mitrani, David Roffe, Alberto Forma, Daniel Levy, Sabeto Yahia, Mordechai Maya, Sabeto Yahia Reva.

Daniel Levy was a medical student at the University of Havana when this picture was taken before a bullet killed him on the deck of the Altalena.

3

SANTOS SUAREZ AND MIRAMAR

My family was what you might call today upwardly mobile. Two years after moving to Old Havana we moved to the suburbs, to Santos Suarez this time. The house where we lived was a triplex that stood on top of a small hill and each apartment had a big square terrace where we would run to every afternoon to catch the elusive tropical breezes. Since air conditioning was still rare in Cuba, most people practically lived in their terraces. That was where we entertained and adjourned to after meals to talk, relax and even to watch television in the cool nights of fall and winter, or under a big ceiling fan in the hot summers. We lived on the third floor and to my amazement and good luck shortly after moving in, a family with two young daughters moved into the second floor, one of which turned out to be one of my classmates.

Shortly after, the city decided to open up the street in order to repave it and until the day we moved away it remained open, with a mountain of stones on one side ready to be used for the construction that never happened. As a result us kids had a wonderful time climbing the "mountain" that became our playground. Since no cars could go by, we had the street all to ourselves and in many summer evenings the neighbors would get together and throw block parties when everybody would bring a different dish and eat in big tables right on the street.

It was a wonderful, simple time when we walked almost anywhere, unafraid and happy. We walked to school, to friends' houses and to the movies. And everywhere we went, we followed the carefully-tended gardens of the suburban homes, mostly two-story town houses adorned with graceful columns and fences.

Unfortunately one day my mother found out that the teacher of Yiddish and *Yiddishe Gesichte* himself, Lerer Gershcovich, had moved to our neighborhood. Lerer Gershcovich had a bad temper and it did not take much to make it flare up, especially if he ran into someone like me, who might very easily forget a line or two of my difficult-to-understand and impossible-to-memorize Yiddish lessons. On occasions like that, his head would turn from side to side, his glasses would slide down his nose, and he would turn beet-red and go into an apoplectic fit, banging his fists on the table. Therefore I lived in constant fear of the blessed gentleman. Imagine my agony when my mother declared one fine morning that I was to walk to school from then on with our new neighbor. Don't ask me how I lived through the first morning. We walked in silence the six blocks to school —he was obviously as annoyed at having to walk me to school as I was at walking with him, and had no interest in engaging me in conversation— and I was praying that he would not hear the rumble in my stomach or the crazy beat of my heart. I never walked so fast in my life and I proceeded to throw up as soon as I got to school. The teacher, upon seeing me enter the classroom pale and trembling, called my mother and explained what had happened and thank God that was the end of my walks with Lerer Gershcovich.

By the time I was fifteen I couldn't wait to go out on my first date. I used to watch my neighbor Sophie's sister, who was older than us, get all dressed up to go out, and listened to my parents' tales of the fabulous cabarets with their magnificent shows, and I imagined a fantastic world just outside my reach full of beautiful music and excitement. Unfortunately my father was extremely strict and the first time I went out on a date I had to double with my cousin Jaime, who acted as de facto chaperon when I went out with his best friend to catch the show at the legendary Tropicana. (Age minimums were not enforced in Cuba. If you looked old enough, you were allowed in any night club in Havana.) The problem was that the show started at ten-thirty and my father wanted me back home by midnight. Considering that it took an hour to drive back to my house we only had time to see half the show before we had to head back, but for years I remembered the excitement of the music, the chorus girls that danced on walkways suspended between tropical trees and the beautiful fountain with the dancing nymphs lit up in a rainbow of colors, that greeted the cars when they circled the driveway of the fabulous nightclub in the outskirts of Havana.

I did not go to my first formal until a year later. In the meantime I joined a Zionist youth movement prompted by Sophie and her sister, who took me with them to the Zionist Union in the

Paseo del Prado, where *Hanoar Hazioni* held their weekly meetings. There we danced Israeli folk dances and learned about the new Jewish state across the sea, but when I found out that they discouraged their members from wearing makeup and dressing up I decided that it was time to go on to other things. This was the early 50's and even though Cuba, like the rest of Latin America, had not participated in the war, it benefited all the same from the post-war boom. Sugar prices were high and tourism was at an all-time high, and growing. Many Jews, as befitted their improved economic situation, had moved to the Northern suburbs of Vedado and Miramar, but most of the synagogues were still in Old Havana. Things were ripe for the construction of a new showplace synagogue-community center. A drive was undertaken to raise funds for that purpose and two years later the Patronato went up on Linea Street, one of the main thoroughfares of El Vedado.

By then we were living in the swanky suburb of Miramar and as part of the inaugural celebrations, the ladies committee decided to organize a debutante ball. All the young girls ages fifteen to sixteen were invited to participate. I had just met a dashing young man at a friend's house, whose family had built an imposing home in the Country Club of Havana. I was sitting in the patio where my friend Ruth was showing a group of us the site where their swimming pool was going to be built, when in walked a young man with her brother. I became mesmerized at the sight of Alex Dessler, who was tall, dark and handsome, and after gathering enough courage, I asked him to be my escort for the ball. When I told my mother he had agreed, she was ecstatic. "I will have the most beautiful gown made for you!" she exclaimed and ran to phone the dressmaker.

SANTOS SUAREZ AND MIRAMAR

Alex was the son of one of the largest garment manufacturers in Havana, and even though his parents had been European immigrants like mine, he went to an American school and socialized mostly with the upper- class American Jews. We, on the other hand were, what you might call, entrenched in middle class. My father was less impressed. "I know he is the son of Hershel Dessler, whom I respect and admire," he said, "but I ask you, who is he?" Genealogy in this case was not impressing my father, but as a rule I was not allowed to date anyone unless he knew who his parents were and was able to conduct an exhausting investigation of the poor unsuspecting boy. I was excited about the party, but worried more about making a graceful entrance in front of all those people, half of which I did not even know.

The fateful day came and when Alex picked me up in a black Corvette with red leather interiors (the only one in Havana) and pinned an orchid corsage on my pink lace dress, I felt like Cinderella riding in her carriage with Prince Charming by her side.

We got to the Patronato, walked up the stairs of the side entrance under the big concrete arches that Manuel Capablanca, one of Havana's top architects, had designed in the shape of the top half of a Jewish star, and came in through a metal door emblazoned with a big Lion of Judah. The beautiful synagogue had recently been inaugurated and the doors were shining brightly when we opened them that winter night. Young girls were scurrying through the hallways leaving behind the scent of *Joy* and *Miss Dior* when I parted with Alex, and was spirited away by a volunteer to the back of the auditorium, where the debutantes were kept hidden. I got lost in a sea of pink and white lace, checked my makeup in a small compact that I carried in my purse and waited anxiously for my name to be called. When I finally came out the applause was louder than anybody's —mostly for Alex, of course, who was standing outside waiting for me in a white dinner jacket and black tuxedo pants, but it felt good all the same. Never mind that I was wearing stockings for the first time in my life as well as a pair of backless high-heel slippers, and almost tripped on the red carpet they had laid out for us, but when I came on stage Alex was there to hold me —all six feet two inches of him—-and only those in the very first rows might have noticed my near fumble which got covered up real fast by my look of adoration at my handsome escort.

That evening started a long romance that would color the rest of my life. I danced the first waltz with my beaming father, who had a hard time letting go of his little girl and I hardly remember the rest of that night, which I spent dancing with my escort in a haze of excitement and nervousness. Two weeks later I was pleasantly surprised when Alex asked me to be his girlfriend and gave me his graduation ring. "I don't want you to date anyone else," he told me as he slipped the blue and gold ring with the crest of the Ruston Academy on my finger. "You're my girl now."

Most of Alex's friends belonged to the American community, a kind of elitist group who kept to themselves. He had two or three close friends and stayed away from the rest, preferring his own company most of the time. On week nights, after he'd drop me home from college, I would sit on the floor of the hallway, where the one telephone we had in our apartment was kept on top of a small black-iron table, and talk with him for hours, sometimes sharing jokes and teen-age confidences, but the prevalent mood about Alex was one of constrained melancholy. He was fun in the company of friends, however as soon as we were alone I was aware of a restlessness that brewed just below the surface of his devil-may-care façade.

Alex was the younger of two brothers and had been born when his parents were older and already established into an extremely social way of life. President Batista himself had been among the close to two hundred people that had come to the inauguration of their new home— including a violin orchestra that flew in from Mexico City especially for the occasion.

There had been very little time for a new child at that stage in the Desslers lives. Alex's mother was without a doubt one of the most elegant women in all Havana. She was tall and slim, with regal bearing, thick auburn hair and shiny alabaster skin that would have put a young girl to shame. As a young woman she had been a dazzling beauty and after marrying Hershel Dessler had settled into the comfortable role of society matron. She was known as the queen of Havana's Jewish society. A role that she played to perfection, chairing committees at the temple and helping to raise funds for the poor — always dressed impeccably for the part. But Dina Dessler was not one to make too much of an effort at anything, not even at being well dressed. She used to keep a mannequin with her measurements at her couturier's and when she needed a new dress, which was often, she would simply call and explain the occasion and a couple of days later her chauffeur would bring home the new creation.

She could be found in the first seat of the synagogue every Friday, facing the imposing *bima* in a new outfit that included matching hat and gloves, her head tilted haughtily towards the wood-paneled walls of the chapel as she appraised the rest of the congregants. Dina Dessler was one of those women who woke up in the morning with every hair in place, always perfectly coifed and made up, and commanded the kind of respect usually reserved for royalty. People kowtowed to her, not only because she was Hershel Dessler's wife, but because her sheer presence demanded respect. She was a perfectionist, and destiny had placed her in the right spot to play that game.

Alex had wanted to take me home to meet his mother, but she always had a reason to refuse. Once because the drapes needed cleaning, another time because the maid was off. Eventually he sneaked me into the house one night after everybody was asleep and brought me up to his room through a black granite spiral staircase. I had never seen a house like that before. The living room was dominated by a bar that took over a whole wall. The front of the bar was a huge fish tank filled with tropical fish in the colors of the rainbow. The coral and vegetation in the bottom created a tropical habitat that was kept glowing at night under low-voltage lighting, lending the room a surrealistic aura in the dark. We kept our voices low as we leaned against the thick glass, and a striped black and white fish looked at me curiously from the safe haven of his watery home. "This is the most popular spot in the whole house," Alex told me smiling his disarming smile. "We always sit here and have a drink before dinner." That statement was foreign to me. My parents didn't drink more than an occasional drink with friends —and rarely at home.

The bar was also were Hershel Dessler entertained his many friends. A warm, well-liked man who always stood ready to help people in need, Hershel Dessler had been instrumental in the building of the new synagogue, but between his businesses and his strong commitment to the community, had also little time for family life. Alex had been brought up by a nanny and in the few occasions when he visited my home he would recoil when he'd see my father suddenly grab me and plant a big noisy kiss on my cheek, as he often did.

"I'm going to die young," he told me one night when we were sitting in his car talking after school, a lock of shiny black hair falling on his forehead, "probably in a car race." He was a car race enthusiast and would often take his Corvette for a spin out on the highway, something that was becoming increasingly dangerous under the prevailing political situation, when anybody, particularly a young man, didn't need much of a reason to be arrested if found after hours outside metropolitan Havana.

These were also the days of Jimmy Dean and many were impressed by the young actor's premature death, so I didn't think much of Alex's death wish and laughed the whole thing off. In any case, it was hard to figure out when he was talking seriously — when he was in town that is, since he would often disappear for several days. It wasn't until much later that I found out those absences where due to his dangerous escapades with the underground. Like many of the young people at the time, Alex wanted a change in the regime and thought nothing of joining the revolutionary forces whenever possible to plant a bomb here or start a demonstration there. Danger for him was part of the excitement, what made the world go round, and since he did not consider life a dear commodity, it was a game he was ready to play.

My friend Suly came into my life when I was sixteen and she a year older. A child survivor of the Holocaust, she had come to Cuba at the age of six. Suly was born in Kovno, and was six months old when the Germans invaded Lithuania. Her family was rounded up, together with the other Jews of Kovno, and taken to the ghetto, where they lived until she was three. Of more than 40,000 people that came into the ghetto of Kovno, only 17,000 survived. Suly's father was in charge of bread distribution and befriended a German officer who tipped him off to the fact that all the children and old people were about to be killed so that they could take the able-bodied survivors to the camps. "Find a way to save your daughter," the German officer told him. "There isn't much time."

Suly was taken out of the ghetto by a rabbi's wife, who had taken off her sheitl (the wig that Orthodox Jewish women wear to cover their hair) and had her own hair cut off in order to pass as a Lithuanian farmer. After giving Suly a sleeping pill, she put her in a sack of potatoes and, with the help of other collaborators, transported her to a ship en route to Palestine, where Suly lived until the age of six with the rabbi, the rabbi's wife, and three other children that the couple had saved. Her parents, who had stayed in the ghetto, were separated by the Germans. Her mother was sent to Stuthold, a camp that was set up in Lithuania and her father went to Dachau. Luckily this happened towards the end of the war and they both survived, albeit with far less flesh on their bones, but alive. After liberation Suly's mother went looking for her husband in Dachau, which having been in Germany, was now in the American side, and they reunited.

Suly's father was truly a lucky man. He had a brother in Cuba, a prosperous industrialist who, as soon as the war was over, flew to Europe to find his brother and his wife and brought them both to Havana. But Suly was still in Israel, a happy six-year old who lived with the rabbi's wife. "I didn't want to leave her," she told me one day, "I thought she was my mother." After much searching they finally tracked down Suly in Jerusalem — she was walking back from the neighborhood market where she had gone to fetch a bottle of milk for her breakfast when they found her, a thoroughly independent, happy little girl— and brought her to Cuba, where she became one of my closest friends.

By the time I met her, Suly was already acclimated to her new home, even though she spoke with an accent —she never stopped rolling her r's, a leftover from her Hebrew— a fact that set her apart from all the other teenagers in our group. She came from a different world, a world very different from mine.

Once Suly's mother was entertaining a friend from Europe when Suly and I walked into their apartment. The women were laughing reminiscing about the times when they were both single. Suly's mother had been an accountant in Lithuania and had had her own life before she married. She and her friend were obviously having fun recalling a time that belonged just to the two of them, before husbands and children came into their lives, which was something unheard of for Cuban women of my mother's generation, who went from their parents' home to their wedding day.

Suly was tall and blonde, and wore her hair straight and short, which gave her an air of sophistication. She looked and acted like a European, went to the American school and drove her own car. She was bright and different. If she was traumatized by her early experiences, she kept it well under wraps. But she did not marry until late in life and as a result never had chil-

dren of her own. Perhaps she was still nurturing her childhood, which had been so cruelly taken away from her by the Nazis.

Summer was beach season, when we would spend glorious, breezy days at our club, which was walking distance from my home. El Casino Deportivo had been built by Jose Hornedo, a Cuban mulatto who did well, as a protest to the ritzy, restricted beach clubs like the Havana Yacht Club that wouldn't allow people of color as members. Neither did they allow Jews. When he built El Casino Deportivo he didn't spare any luxuries and opened it to everyone, regardless of color, race or religion that could pay the modest monthly fee. As a result Jews became one of the new club's main patrons.

It was there, in the opulent red and green rooms —big halls entirely covered in red and green marble— that we would gather among the imposing round marble columns, sitting in wood and cane rocking chairs that faced the sea through tall, half-moon-topped glass French doors. On Saturday nights a band would play in a corner of the wide granite terrace fenced in by a stone balustrade, where couples danced under the stars, lulled by the caress of the soft ocean breezes. There were squash courts and big halls with tables to play cards and dominoes, and a big seawall that encroached on the blue-green waters of the Atlantic, taming them and allowing us to swim in a natural pool. During summer vacation I walked every day from my home to El Casino with the sea in the distance and the soothing sound of the water lapping at the rocky littoral as my constant companion. I loved to go down the barnacle-encrusted steps to the cool bottle-green waters that, smelling of all the riches of the sea, ebbed and flowed under the bridge, and swim all the way to the end, where a small beach had been carved out of the rocks. Life proceeded at a gentle, happy pace and I dreamt the hopeful dreams of a sixteen year old.

4

HAIM

The last thing that Haim Tuchman saw when he left Chelem was a patch of white. Long after the tearful good-byes at the train station had faded from his consciousness, he sat in the tiny train compartment, immobilized by the cold.

Outside, the town where he had spent his first twenty years laid covered by a pristine blanket of snow. The white, icy helmet was punched here and there by hopeful sprouts that would soon surrender to new snow, and as the train sped through the desolate fields, he was swept up by an inexplicable yearning. But after a few pensive moments he started to laugh. As the white vastness spread out before him, the irony of the image finally hit him. He closed his eyes and let the new, light feeling of freedom spread slowly through his body. He sat up, braced himself and felt it warm every single nerve ending, as the tension that had cramped his muscles just a few moments before started to disappear, for he finally realized that what he was really yearning for was the familiarity of the cold —the only environment he really knew. As he looked out the tiny window he readied himself to leave all that behind and wondered what would take its place. Some steamy tropical jungle? A forgotten village in the middle of nowhere perhaps?

His whole family had come to the train station for the send-off. A furrier by trade, Moshe Aaron Tuchman had three sons and four daughters and had taken in a young nephew when his brother died, so when all were still together in Poland there were eight children in the Tuchman household. Now that the boys were nearing military age, he had insisted that they should leave the country. Jews were not allowed to study the professions and when enlisted in the Polish Army, they were assigned only the worst and most dangerous posts. Haim had his heart set on becoming a doctor, and saw little future for himself in Poland, where medical school was off-limits to Jews. There was no question that the boys had to be the first to leave. Behind were left Esther, Mindle, Hannah and Sonia, with the promise that they too would soon come to Cuba. One of the girls, Gitel, who was married, and the older brother Jacob, were already there and the younger son, Fishel, had his papers in order. Haim kissed each one of the girls on the cheek, and his mother last and when he walked away from his father's embrace to climb up the first step into the departing train, he felt a bulge in his trouser pocket. He put his hand in and found a wad of paper money. He took it out and found twenty dollar bills carefully folded and a piece of paper with the words: *"Gei gesunt."* Moshe Aaron Tuchman was letting go of another one of his sons, without any assurances that he would ever see him again.

It took two more trains to get from Warsaw to Hamburg,

from where the Tropicale had sailed for Cuba. Now, as he approached Havana Harbor, Haim was surrounded by a soft palette of acquas and greens. The bluegreen waters of the Atlantic that hours before had clashed angrily against the majestic transatlantic, now reflected the misty blue of dawn. All that remained from the turbulence of the last three days was an occasional patch of seaweed that surfaced here and there in the wake of the ship.

By the time Haim got his first glimpse of Morro Castle, the old lighthouse that guarded the port, the ocean had become calmer and cleaner, until it acquired a dark green cast, not unlike the color of the meadows outside his tiny Polish village in the spring. And when the palm-lined avenues of Havana finally came into view, he felt well enough to be able to smell the salt in the warm fresh air and feel the caress of the tropical sun on his weary face. Years later Haim would remember that moment as the time when he fell hopelessly in love with Cuba.

The line at the big customs buildings was long and slow, and Haim took his jacket off, draping it over one shoulder as his arms started itching under the thick wool. Next he loosened the knot of his tie and wiped out the beads of perspiration that had started to form on his forehead as he tried to shade his eyes from the sun. The salty smell of the harbour mixed with the odor of cigar smoke and sweat as people tried to push their way through the crowd looking for relatives and lost luggage.

Twenty minutes later he found himself in front of an immigration agent. The man looked sleepily up at Haim, pushed away a thick leather-bound old book and extended his hand for the passport.

"Nombre?"

"Haim. Haim Tuchman"

"*Jaime,*" the man answered, giving the name the Spanish pronunciation. "Jaime Tuchman". And he wrote that name in an official looking document, stamped it and gave it back to Haim.

"*Buena suerte,*" he said finally. "Good luck". And he smiled wearily as he motioned for the next passenger to get closer.

Haim took the passport and walked away briskly from the customs area. His brother Jacob was supposed to have met him at the harbor, but he had been held up at the nearby town of San Nicolas, where his wife was giving birth to their second child. He had made this clear when he heard the date of arrival, telling him not to wait if he did not see him at the harbor, for there was a strong possibility that the dates of his arrival and that of the delivery would coincide.

Haim stood in front of the harbor and looked around. No sign of Jacob, and he thought that if a baby was being born that day, it had to be a good omen.

At either side of him a wide ribbon of cement cut the waters of the Atlantic that sprayed him with a soft mist, while a cool breeze started to dry off the sweat on his chest and neck. Feeling better, he started to walk away from the harbor, but as he ventured into the city streets the intensity of the sun became overwhelming and he stopped at a small park to catch his breath. Before him a bronze statue of a Spanish caballero mounted on a horse faced the sea. Haim sat on a bench under a giant ceiba tree and was suddenly taken aback by the abundant greenery that surrounded him.

A young couple strolled by, hand in hand, and sat in the bench across from him, engrossed in what sounded like playful conversation. The words intrigued him, but he recognized the smiles and the glances. He looked away uncomfortably, not wanting to intrude in their privacy, but the sound of laughter made him look again.

They were staring at his feet, and he realized that he had boots on. They must look really out of place in this weather, he thought, smiling self-consciously, gathered his belongings and kept on walking, promising himself that he would buy a pair of white shoes with his very first paycheck.

He walked for another five minutes before turning into one of the narrow, cobblestone side streets, where two and three-story balconied buildings crowded next to one another. The smell of fresh laundry made him look up at one of the black-iron-railed balconies and he saw a young woman hanging a white shirt on a clothes line. She had long, dark hair that she wore loose around her shoulders and as Haim got closer, he realized that she was about his age.

"*Hola*", he ventured to say waving his hand up in the air and the sun felt warm against his cheek.

"*Hola,*" she answered leaning against the railing to get a better look at the fresh-faced blonde youth, and as she smiled he realized that she had small, even teeth that looked even smaller within her full lips.

He started to smile back when a singsong caught his ear. "*Tengo mango, mango del Caney, mamey colorado*". (I have mango, mango from Caney, red mamey.) A street vendor was intoning his litany, the street *pregones* as he pushed a cart full of the strangest fruit Haim had ever seen. He got closer to the cart, fascinated by the fruit as much as by the man, for he was black, the color of ebony, and Haim had never seen a black man before. The man stopped the cart and his bounty glimmered in the sun. There were pineapples, mangoes, zapotes, anones, the succulent fruits were laid out in the cart like exotic birds caught in midflight.

Haim pointed hesitantly to a brown, conical fruit that had been sliced on one side to reveal a sole, shiny black pit surrounded by orangey red meat.

"Here, have a piece of mamey," the man said and cut a fresh slice that he offered to Haim with a smile, his teeth startingly white against his dark face as he cleaned his knife against a piece of white cloth. As Haim bit into the red sweet meat, it slid slowly from the skin to melt into his mouth and he nodded his pleasure to the vendor, who pointed next to a bright yellow mango, and then to a green, prickly guanabana which he pulled apart with his fingers to reveal its white, luscious meat. Haim tasted a piece of each, reveling in the exotic taste. Finally he took out a coin from one of his pockets and gave it to the black man, who put it away as he eyed a curvy mulatto girl sashaying down the street. "Girl, if you cook the way you walk, I'll clean up my plate," he yelled at her with an appreciative smile while he pushed the cart in front of him. The woman answered with a disdainful glance and a half smile before hurrying up down the street.

Haim watched this exchange without understanding fully what was said. He had learned a little Spanish before embarking on the trip and knew that it had something to do with food, but the full meaning of the words eluded him and he couldn't understand why the woman was half smiling, even though she seemed upset. The subtleties of flirting, Cuban style, were still a mystery to him.

He kept walking, and by the time he got to the next intersection it became clear that he was lost. He was looking for Zulueta Street, where someone on the boat had said he could find cheap accommodations. "All the same," he thought, "I might as well enjoy it." He kept walking, admiring the graceful lines of the Havana Cathedral, with its twin bell towers and curlicues. The closest thing he had seen was the big city hall in Warsaw, but that had been half-covered with snow —instead of shining in the sun, like the baroque façade of the cathedral was now. Half a block later a series of massive columns set between graceful arches supported an ample portal in front of what looked like a big government building, and he decided that was a good place to find some shade and rest for a few minutes.

A few feet away he saw a green awning with the words *Cafe de Armas* written on it. He came in, took off his jacket and sat on a stool, letting his elbows rest on the cool marble counter before stretching his arms, that were getting tired of hauling his suitcase through the city streets. He took out the crumpled piece of paper where he had written down the directions to the boarding house and showed it hesitantly to the waiter. The man looked at it with a puzzled expression, said a few words in Spanish to another customer, then to Haim and laughed out loud.

"*Una cuadra*", he said, pointing to the right, "one block away from here," and sized him up as he returned the paper. "*Parece polaco*," he said to another customer. "*Luce que se acaba de bajar del barco*."

"He looks like a Polack, seems like he just got off the boat". Haim straigtened up in his seat, picked up his suitcase, thanked the waiter and found his way out. All he understood of that exchange was the word *polaco*.

"Well, at least he got that one right," he said to himself chuckling at the irony. He had dreamt of becoming a doctor, but the Polish university where he had to enrol would not allow Jews in that faculty. His only avenue at his age was to either join the Polish army or become a tradesman and earn a meager living in his little *shtetl* like his father had. He had opted to leave instead. "In Poland I was called a Jew and here I'm called a Polack," he mused, and wondered if he would ever really belong to his new adoptive country.

By the time Haim got to Zulueta Street it was way after noon. He spotted the building in a corner. It must have been white in some distant past, but now the old city dust that burrowed in its crevices lent it a dark gray cast that blended harmoniously with the surroundings. He went up the narrow staircase. There was a hallway at the top, where an old woman was seated behind a small desk adding figures in a book. She looked up at him and after a short inspection asked:

"*¿Quiere un cuarto?*" "Do you want a room?"

Haim recognized the word, his friend had written it down in the piece of paper next to the Yiddish word *shtimer* for room, and quickly nodded yes. She got up slowly, leaning against the table for support and led him through a courtyard planted with ferns and hibiscus to a small room in the back.

"Fifty cents a day," she said, and demanded payment for the first two days before showing him to the room. "It will be quiet", she said, "*Tranquilo*".

Haim came in, put down his suitcase on the floor and surveyed his new accomodations. A small cot was placed against the wall. The only other pieces of furniture were a small night table and a commode with a chair. "Not much," he thought, but for the time being at least it was home.

He sat down on the bed and suddenly realized how far away he was from everyone he knew. He thought of Mindle and wondered how long it would take to get papers for her and her family. His middle sister had married five years before and had a four-year old daughter who was the light of Haim's life. She was also expecting another baby. Little Shosh would come to him every night after dinner, put her fat little arms around his neck and ask for a bedtime story. Haim would take her on his back for a ride and, giggling and laughing they would both ride up the stairs to her bedroom where he would sit and tell her stories until reluctantly she would close her eyes and go to sleep.

Her favorite bedtime story was Simbad and time and again she would ask him when she would be able to go in a big boat across the sea like the famous sailor. Soon, he would tell her. Soon we will all go across the ocean to a far away place where the sun always shines. Oh, how he missed his mother's constant shuffling in the kitchen, the home-cooked meals that him and his brothers and sisters shared every evening. The constant arguing and carryings on of a big family.

He had been the third one to leave and he would make sure that the others followed. He had promised Mindle and Hannah. Little Hannah still had stars in her eyes. She wanted more than anything to come to America and be in the theater. She had a beautiful voice and had already appeared in a couple of school plays. With her lithe figure and angelic face she had her heart set on a career in the stage.

The day he left she had taken him aside and made him promise to send for her as soon as he could. "I'm not marrying anybody here," she had said, "I'm going to America. Please Haim, make sure you send for me as soon as you can. Promise me!" she had begged, putting to good use her innate dramatic flair. And he had promised. So many things were riding now on that promise. He was barely twenty and it seemed that the weight of the world was resting on his young shoulders. But slowly he bowed down to exhaustion and finally fell into a restless sleep.

He woke up to a room full of light that was streaming in through the sheer curtains and realized he had been asleep for twelve hours. The back of his shirt was soaked with perspiration and there was a wet patch on the sheet where he had fallen asleep.

He got up, opened the tiny window and looked out. The street was already teeming with vendors, streetcars and an occasional car. And even though it was still early, the bright sun made everything look clean and sharp. As far as his eyes could see every street led to the sea that surrounded the city in a ribbon of blue. In the distance an island of greenery cut through the old buildings leading to a seaside promenade. "That must be the Paseo del Prado," he said, unfolding a map of Havana that he had brought with him from Poland as he luxuriated in the early morning sun. He stretched, trying to chase away the last traces of sleep, put on his shoes, selected a change of clothes and walked the length of the hallway to the bathroom.

There was a stall shower, a toilet and a coarse terry towel hanging from a hook on the wall. Haim showered, dried himself up and made a mental note to buy a towel. He then put on a clean shirt and a new pair of pants, combed back his thick blonde hair and went down to the corner cafe where a few customers were already seated sipping steaming cups of coffee and reading the morning paper.

The waiter wiped his hands on his white apron, took one look at Haim and branded him a foreigner. His pink cheeks, blonde hair, even his clothes gave him away. He greeted Haim, pulled up a narrow wooden chair and pointed to a marble-topped small round table. Haim sat down, asked for *desayuno* and was brought a cup of steaming *cafe con leche* and a crusty piece of buttered bread.

He looked around him and saw a man dipping the buttered bread into the coffee. Haim took the bread and did the same, watching the butter form concentric circles on the receding foam of the milk as the bread soaked up the liquid. He bit on the coffee-flavored bread and emptied what remained in the cup. Not bad, he thought, as he wiped his lips with a napkin while he motioned the waiter to refill his cup, which he quickly drained. He paid for breakfast, got up and left the cafe.

All he needed now was a job, and he patted the tiny piece of paper he had kept hidden in the upper pocket of his jacket all the way from Poland, along with the twenty dollars that his father had managed to scrape together as a parting gift.

He had a name and an address and he set out to El Cerro, to find Motl Kantor.

Grandfather Máximo (right) selling ties in Havana circa 1926.

Far left: The Capitolio,
a small replica of the one
in Washington, D.C.

Left: A "solar" in Old Habana

Left, down: The old Centro
Gallego, today's Palace of
Fine Arts, was built during
the booming 1920's.

Right: The Patronato, main
synagogue of Havana

Down: Observant jews
reading the Torah in
today's Havana.

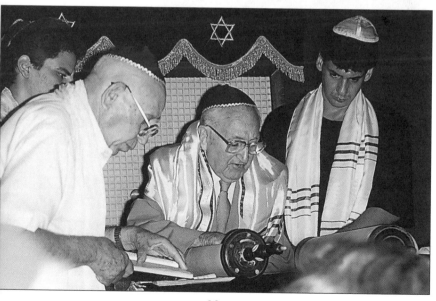

Today's revolutionary Cuba still worships the heroes of the revolution.

The Cathedral of Havana.

Detail of the ceiling of the Hotel Inglaterra in Old Havana.

5

EL CERRO

El Cerro had been one of the swankiest neighborhoods in Havana at the turn of the century, but it had seen better days and now it had turned into a working class district. The Calzada, its main drag, was lined with townhouses separated by Greek columns that lent an air of elegance to an otherwise nondescript neighborhood where good, honest people toiled daily to earn a modest living. The hub of El Cerro was the commercial district where a hodgepodge of small stores and cafes faced the cable-car depot. This was the center of the network that criscrossed Havana, transporting passengers all over the city, and the only means of public transportation at the time.

The sign on the wall of the small store read *Los Dos Hermanos* (The Two Brothers) and in the window there were all sorts of men, women and children's apparel, from shoes to clothes and custom jewelry, displayed without any particular attention to detail. Inside, a middle-aged man was showing a customer a pair of shoes. He wore glasses and the back of his small frame had the curvature of someone who had spent a lifetime bent over boxes of merchandise. In the corner, a salesgirl was cutting a piece of brown wrapping paper from a big roll. Haim went straight to the man.

"Gut morgen," he said in yiddish. " Good morning. I just arrived from Poland and I'm looking for Motl Kantor".

"That would be me," answered the man, closing the lid on a shoebox and giving it to the salesgirl. "Concha, wrap these up for Mrs. Aguilar, please." And then turning to Haim, "What can I do for you young man?"

"My sister Gitel wrote to me and told me perhaps you had a job for me?"

"You're Gitel's brother? "the man said looking appreciatevely at the young man in front of him, as a smile started to spread slowly over his face. "Of course, we have been expecting you."

"My brother Jacob was supposed to have met my boat, but he was held up in San Nicolas..."

"Yes, yes, I heard the good news. *Mazel tov*. I understand it's another boy. Come here, let me look at you. He said, adjusting his glasses. Tell me what you can do."

"Well, I'm a hard worker and I've taught myself a little Spanish. See...?" said Haim, producing a small dictionary from his pants pocket.

Motl smiled at the young man. He looked well cared for. His shirt was of coarse material, but clean and his eyes shone with an eagerness that reminded Motl of his own young years.

"Can you lift boxes and climb stairs?"

"Of course I can!"

"Good, you got yourself a job. I need somebody to put some order in the stock room. Two pesos a day. Half a day on *Shabbes*."

Haim came in early the next day, greeted his new employer with a big smile and went straight to work in the back. The room was dark except for a big window next to the ceiling and the walls were painted light green to keep the temperature down. There were stacks of boxes laid out all over the floor, some of them half open and Haim spent the morning organizing them according to sizes, content and color. He only stopped around eleven when Concha, the salesgirl, brought him a tiny cup of Cuban coffee. "For energy," she had said, "Manuel at the corner cafe brews it so it can lift a dead man!" Haim emptied the tiny cup and asked for another. He was acquiring his first Cuban vice.

By the end of the morning the shoe boxes were piled up neatly against one wall. The shirts and pants were on another and he had tagged the boxes with a thick black pen, leaving an aisle in the middle. He was done around noon and had started to sweep up the room when Motl came in. Motl Kantor looked around apreciatively and his eyes lit up as he surveyed the isles of merchandise neatly piled and tagged.

"Now we can call this a stockroom," he said putting his arms around Haim. The boy's handsome features were covered with perspiration and he still held a broom in one hand, but a smile of satisfaction spread over his face. "Wait till my Sorele takes a look at this," said Motl taking off his glasses to clean them with a piece of chamois he kept in his pants pocket, "and by the way, you should start calling me by my Spanish name, Maximo."

"Maximo," Haim said, taking special care to stop at the "x", which was difficult for him to pronounce, and repeated it a few times until he got it right.

"Good, that's almost perfect. Now, tell me something, when was the last time you had a home-cooked meal?" asked Maximo and Haim shrugged, while visions of chicken soup with dumplings danced before his eyes.

"Come, you'll have lunch with us. My Sara is one of the best cooks in all Havana."

They walked along the Calzada, stopping here and there to greet acquantainces of Maximo's and once to buy a lottery ticket from a street vendor, who carried the big *billetes* on his back, until they arrived at a big patio with a few small buildings in the back.

"Come on," said the older man, pointing to a two story building with a small staircase in the front. "It's only one flight up."

The soft aroma of a roast wafted all the way down to the first floor landing, which was covered in a colorful red, blue and white tile in a Moorish design. They climbed the steep staircase and a young servant girl opened the apartment door. A small sitting room covered in red brocade led to the dining room, which looked out to a big terrace.

"This is really where I live, said Maximo, opening the door that led to a big rooftop in the middle of which stood a gazebo with two hammocks hanging on each side. The roof commanded a view of the surrounding buildings all the way down to the Calzada del Cerro.

"After work I come here to feed the pigeons and watch the sun go down. We have beautiful sunsets in Havana."

"Motl, come on in, food's getting cold," a woman's voice called at them. *"Kum, kum, me darfst essen."*

A heavy-set middle-aged woman was standing in the doorway. She was prematurely gray and wore her hair pulled back in an elegant bun. Her fine milky complexion crinkled around her blue eyes in a sprinkling of tiny lines as she greeted them with a smile tempered by curiosity. *"Sheine bojer,"* she said, wiping her hands in the apron that she had tied around her flower-print dress to take a closer look at Haim. "Good looking boy."

"Good Shabes," she said as he came back into the apartment. "Welcome to our home."

Behind her a young woman was carrying a small tray with two glasses of sherry wine. She was about eighteen, with wavy dark-brown hair, semitic features and wide, almond-shaped green eyes framed by thick dark eyebrows. Her nose was the only dissonant feature in an otherwise striking face, but the end result was an air of quiet elegance. She was wearing a white crepe dress that accentuated her voluptuous figure, as it slid over her smooth olive skin.

"This is my daughter Paulina," said Maximo noticing the young man's interest.

"How do you do?" Haim asked somewhat self-consciously, as the girl handed him a glass of wine.

"L'chaim," said Maximo raising his glass. "And good Shabbes. This is Haim Tuchman, Gitele's brother. He's working with me at the store," he told the two women as they sat down on the sofa. "He just reorganized the whole stock room. You should see what it looks like now , Sorele." And then, turning to Haim: "My wife has been after me for years to clean up that room, but I never seem to have enough time."

"I'm very happy you came along young man," said Sara, "we can certainly use someone like you around here." And she gave a meaningful look to her daughter before returning to the kitchen.

"When did you get here?" Paulina asked shyly after her mother had left the room. Even though she was a striking woman, Paulina was self-conscious, particularly with strangers. She was self-effacing and quiet where her mother was strong and affable. Sara's presence could be felt in a room the moment she walked in, usually carrying something good to eat, but at times it felt overwhelming to her young daughter.

"I got here last Thursday," answered Haim. "I left Poland two weeks ago and have been traveling ever since. Stopped at Hamburg and London on the way here," he added, stopping for emphasis on both names, trying to appear worldly.

"You're going to have to learn Spanish if you're going to stay for a while," said Paulina, ignoring his reference to foreign ports, her shyness overcome by the blonde good looks of the young stranger at whom she had been staring ever since he had come into the room.

"I know," said Haim returning her stare. "But I'm gonna need someone to teach me." They had been conversing in Yiddish, the common language of the immigrants and it stroke him as funny that hers was punctuated with a strong Spanish accent.

"Why are you smiling like that," asked Paulina, "did I say something funny?"

"It's not what you say, it's how you say it. You speak Yiddish with a Cuban accent. I've never heard that before."

"You would too," she answered haughtily, picking up the empty glasses "if you would have come here when you were seven." And proceeded towards the dining room without taking another look at him.

The table was set over a pristine lace tablecloth and a big *challah* was placed in the middle, its golden crust gleaming against a small, filigreed silver tray. Maximo sliced a piece of bread for each of them and after a short blessing the maid served the chicken soup with *kreplach*. When they had finished with the soup Paulina brought out the veal roast and Haim ate hungrily, for he had not had a good meal in days.

"I had forgotten how good food can taste," he told Sara, "does your daughter cook as well as you do?"

"She baked the dessert," Sara answered and served him a big slice of honey cake.

"Mm... sweet as honey," he said tasting a piece as he looked teasingly at Paulina. The tea was served in dainty glass cups and Sara placed a lump of sugar in her mouth through which she started sipping the brew. "You must be from Russia," said Haim bemused, "my mother used to tell me that her grand-mother, who was Russian, used to drink tea the same way, but I never saw anybody do it before!". *"Epes,"* answered Sara and continued drinking her tea unperturbed, stopping to savor every sip as it slid through the sugar lump.

Maximo lit up a cigar, and the subtle aroma filled the room as he puffed on the hand-rolled Cuban leaf. Outside, the birds were feasting on bread crumbs, perched on the side of the gaze-bo, as a soft breeze ruffled their feathers in the midday sun.

"The best in the world," said Maximo to Haim as he inhaled, rolling the cigar between thumb and forefinger. "This is really a wonderful country. You should get to know the people here. Tell you what, there is a party at the Centro Israelita next Sunday. Why don't you go with Paulina. There is going to be a lot of young people there. I'm sure you'll enjoy yourselves."

The fans were whirring softly from the eight-foot ceiling,

blending the smell of jasmine from a hundred corsages as Haim and Paulina walked into the big hall of the Centro Israelita that Sunday afternoon.

All week long, as he toiled in the back room, bringing out boxes of shoes as they were needed and rearranging them in an orderly fashion, Haim thought of nothing but this day. He had bought a second-hand radio and every night, as soon as he came from work he would listen to the sensuous rhythms that came out of the brown wooden box. The music fascinated him. From his very first day on the island the myriad colors and sounds had enveloped him in a brilliant cocoon of sensuality that now had become a central component of his life. The rhythms of the city could be felt everywhere. That all-encompassing blend of Afro and Spanish music that rocked the hips of statuesque mulatto women in exclusive cabarets and folksy open-air bandstands had already overflowed from the tiny island to move the rest of the world in a cadence of sultry melodies.

The bolero, the danzon, the rumba were being danced in ballrooms from Paris to New York, from Hamburg to Vienna. He had heard the very first tune aboard the ship as he sneaked up one night from steerage into the first-class ballroom and had promised himself that he would dance to it someday. Now he stood facing the radio and allowed himself to be enveloped by the sound. One-two-three... he moved his feet slowly. One-two-three... slowly his body responded, catching the melody until it started moving automatically to the tune of the song and at last he abandoned himself to the sheer pleasure of the music, whirling round and around the tiny room.

He had brought Paulina a corsage of miniature roses when he had picked her up and she had pinned it on the neckline of her orchid moiré dress. Her hair was swept up and away from her forehead, dark eyebrows framing her blue eyes that shone with a special light this afternoon. Special enough for him to take a second look before offering his arm for her to lean on. Now as they entered the big hall through rows of potted arecca palms, their fronds spread out fan-like against the wall, he thought he and Paulina made a handsome couple and decided that the new white suit he had bought with his first paycheck had been worth every penny. With his blonde hair slicked back and tamed with Vaseline, his dark eyebrows framing big hazel eyes, he was as attractive a man as any that had set foot on the ball room of the Centro Israelita.

"May I have the honor of this dance?" he asked Paulina with exaggerated formality after she had greeted two girlfriends that stood giggling against a wall next to one of the balconies as they looked furtively at Haim, and led her confidently across the room where groups of couples had already started to form. The granite dance floor had been shined to perfection for the party and the tall-ceilinged hall was rendered cozy by an abundance of palms that lined practically every wall. The notes of "*Perfidia*" filled the air and he took a few awkward steps as he held Paulina, but slowly started swaying to the music and felt her relax in his arms as he guided her through the dance floor, mimicking the movements of the other couples, that were sliding gracefully through the big room.

Every once in a while one of the dancers would greet Paulina and look curiously at Haim, who would nod self-consciously, but soon his awkwardness disappeared and he started throwing in a few steps of his own, always in rhythm with the tune, and when the band stopped playing he joined the others in heartfelt applause.

"Who taught you how to dance?" asked Paulina, who stood dumbfounded in the middle of the dance floor, fingering a strand of pearls that shone beguilingly around her neck.

"The same person who is going to teach me Spanish," he said as he circled her waist with his arm once again. "You just gave me my first lesson."

6

PAULINA

Most of the young men Paulina Kantor knew were sons of immigrants like her. The ones she was allowed to date, that is, for gentiles had been all right to befriend at school, but dating them was out of the question. Sara had made sure that fact had been drummed into her head practically from the very first moment she could reason. She wanted her daughter to marry within the faith.

Sara herself had come to Cuba as a young bride. She and Maximo had married in Lithuania, where his family had run a successful glassware business for several generations. Maximo was an avid card player and had come to America to get a fresh start after incurring some serious gambling debts that had cost him his livelihood. Sara had stayed behind with Paulina and her brother Moshe, who were then six and three.

When he first came to Cuba Maximo worked as a peddler, selling belts and ties in the streets. He would carry his wares in a big wooden box that he wore strapped around his shoulders and set it down on the sidewalk, where customers would come and gather around to inspect the merchandise. Pictures of the time show a handsome, debonair young man, dressed in light-colored linens and wearing a straw hat cocked at an angle, a cigarette in a holder dangling from his lips. I suppose that alone in Cuba, making the acquaintance of other young men who came looking to make their fortune like himself, must have felt more like an adventure than a hardship. In the evenings, he shared a room in the house of another immigrant. His one meal of the day, which he ate with the family, was included in the rent. The only other expense he had was break-fast, which cost him ten cents and consisted of a steaming cup of *cafe con leche* and buttered crusty Cuban bread, and since he could have refills of coffee, he always had two cups to last him through the day. The rest of what he made he saved. Six months later, by the time he sent for his wife and children, he already had a small store in El Cerro.

From the very first day Sara had worked with him at the store. She enjoyed dealing with people, and customers would line up to be waited on by "Sarita" as they would affectionate-ly call the good-natured young woman with the milky white complexion that spread over wide slavic cheekbones, and couldn't help but being startled by her big blue eyes. They would often mistake her for a Galician, the fair women of Northern Spain, until her thick Eastern European accent would give her away.

Sometimes Paulina would look at her mother and wondered about her ancestors. Sara certainly did not look Jewish and she had heard once that her maternal grandfather had been killed in a brawl with a Cossack after having too much to drink.

Whether it was true or not she could not tell for sure, for her mother would never confirm it, but this was something completely out of character for a Jewish man as she knew them. In any case her mother looked more like a Lithuanian farmer than a Jewess from a *shtetl*.

Sara was a strict *baleboste,* a real Jewish homemaker, and Paulina had a set routine that included school and chores around the house. Even after they could afford a young maid, Paulina was expected to tidy up her bedroom and help clear up the table. Sara helped in the store and cooked all meals.

The arrangement had proven satisfactory, particularly since Paulina abhorred cooking. She enjoyed busying herself around the house and rarely stepped into the store, which she considered alien territory. "Go make yourself pretty," her mother would tell her, "we'll take care of business." But considering there were no more than a few thousand Jews in all of Cuba and significantly less of marrying age, Paulina's social life was somewhat restricted. She and her cousins Lilia and Rafaela would attend the mixers at the Centro Israelita, where her choices were limited to the local Jewish boys. But most of the young men she knew were by now pretty insular having, like her, grown up in the island.

Nothing, in short, had prepared her for someone like Haim. His tales of the old country, that had bored her to death when recounted by her parents over the Sabbath table now became fascinating stories of a winter wonderland when told by Haim, and his description of London and Hamburg filled her with a longing she could not yet understand.

They would often sit out in the terrace when he would come to visit after work and talk well into the night. Every night he

107

would open a new window through which her small world slowly expanded and every night, as his tale unraveled, she would get a little closer to him. He told her about his parents, and the four sisters that had stayed behind and how he intended to bring them all to America, one by one. Gitele she already knew through some of her father's businesses, since Maximo had a partnership with her and her husband in their country store. Gitele and Jacob, who had left his growing family for a couple of days to see his younger brother, had already come from the provinces to meet him and they had had a wonderful day reminiscing about home and formulating plans for the day when the whole family could be reunited in Cuba.

Maximo had come to Cuba with two brothers. The oldest, Jaime, ran a dry cleaning plant in Old Havana and Eli, the youngest, was his partner in the store. Eli had gotten an American visa and emigrated to Chicago shortly after coming to Cuba, but after having lived in Havana, he missed the easy life of the island and promptly came back. Eli lived with Maximo, and Sara; and Paulina and her brother became his surrogate children. This arrangement proved so satisfactory that he never got married, preferring instead to bask in the warmth of the Kantors' household. Paulina was his favorite niece and she clearly adored him. The Kantors became comfortably settled in Havana and came to form part of the tightly-knit social circle that formed the incipient Jewish community.

Haim and his brothers and sister on the other hand, still had family in Poland and were growing increasingly anxious in view of the growing tide of antisemitism that had started to spread throughout Europe. Ironically, in spite of its best efforts, Cuba was destined to play a crucial role in the wave of refugees that had started to flood American shores. Geography had placed the small island in the crossroads of two worlds and history would throw thousands of displaced souls in its path, forcing it to deal with history in its own terms.

On July of 1936 American authorities proposed that Cuba, due to its strategic location open its doors to 100,000 German Jews, but the announcement aroused bitter antisemitic comments in the Cuban press and the proposal was quickly dropped. A year later the Joint Distribution Committee created the Jewish Relief Committee in Havana to aid the steady stream of refugees that had started to come to Cuba. Every new day brought hundreds, sometimes as many as five hundred people to the small, understaffed office of the JDC looking for money to live on and information on how to get to the United States or bring relatives into Cuba. Haim, Gitel and Jacob now looked anxiously into ways to bring in the rest of the family when Haim got a letter from Hannah.

"I'll read it to you. I haven't even opened it yet," he said to Paulina excitedly as he settled into a chair in the Kantors' living room. "I can't wait for you to meet her," and started to read out loud:

"Dear Haim:

I'm not allowed to go to singing lessons anymore. Mame thinks it's too risky." He stopped and kept reading silently.

"Haim, tell me what it says," said Paulina getting closer. He cleared his throat and kept on reading:

"There's a lot of unrest in the town. Troops are coming through every day. They say they're getting ready for the Germans. Are they really that bad?"

"Ever since you're gone all we talk about is war. I'm scared Haimele, I wish you were here.

His voice trailed off, he put down the letter and looked up at Paulina. There were tears in his eyes. The dashing young man she had fallen in love with, who feared nothing, now looked at her for an answer.

"It's not like her to be scared," Paulina. "I must do something to get her out of there. My God, how can I even think of my own happinness at a time like this. If anything happens to any of them, I'll never forgive myself!"

"Darling, what can you do?"

"I must go back and get them out of there!"

"Are you out of your mind? People are trying to get out any way they can. You'll never make it back. We have to find a way to get them out, but I believe we have a better chance from here."

"But how?" he asked, brushing back his thick blonde hair with both hands.

"Father will start asking around. He has friends in the *yishuv*, even some in the government. We'll do all we can."

But Paulina's good wishes were to meet with some opposition. Back in 1938 the entire world was mired in a deep recession. Influential segments of the Cuban economy now demanded an end to the flood of Jewish immigrants for fear that they would take jobs away from the natives. That same situation had prompted President Roosevelt to curtail immigrant visas for Jewish refugees who were trying to enter the United States. Haim was thankful to be in Cuba and to have a job. He was a likable young man and Maximo Kantor had taken him under his wing, but after Hannah's letter he could think of nothing else but to bring the rest of his family to Cuba.

Sitting in his small travel agency, Zaide D'Gabriel felt restless. He catered mostly to the Jewish community in Havana and that morning he had had a meeting with Juan J. Remus, the Cuban Secretary of State. Remus had been brutally honest when he handed D'Gabriel a handful of landing permits. "They are going to exterminate the last Jew in Europe. Why don't you do something about it?" he had told him. The permits had been issued by Manuel Benitez. The new Minister of Immigration sold them for $150 each, but some permits were granted free of charge to D'Gabriel, who gave them periodically to *Haia*s, the Jewish Relocation Agency in New York.

Ever since his morning meeting, D'Gabriel could think of nothing else. If he could only intercede, do something to help. The devastation in Europe kept escalating, but from his position in Cuba he felt utterly helpless. Other than handing out a few free permits, there was little he could do. The Jewish organizations in Cuba were small and had no political influence. American Jews, on the other hand, were known to be powerful. D'Gabriel decided to send a telegram to a well-positioned relative in New York and got himself invited to a symposium of the top American Jewish organizations that was going to be held in that city.

Fourteen organizations met in New York that May to devise strategies and take measures against the growing wave of anti-semitism that was sweeping the world. The agenda of the day was what advise to dispense to German Jews so that they could keep their possessions. D'Gabriel asked to be heard, and courageously requested American help in order to maintain Cuba within the chain of relief, proposing to take the power away from Benitez's hands and have the visas issued through the Secretary of State instead. But Cuba was a small country, and the Jewish community negligible. His request was ignored. He went to a Yiddish language newspaper in New York and asked them to publish a story about the strategic importance of Cuba in saving Jewish lives, but again his request was not granted. In the end he came back to Cuba dispirited and empty-handed.

In the meantime Benitez's business fluorished. Hapag-Lloyd, a German shipping company known today as Hamburg American Line, bought permits for two full cruiseships. The company was to sell a travel package with Benitez's permits for two of their ships, the St. Louis and the Flandre that were going to sail for Cuba in mid May.

As the sailing time got closer, Benitez's fortune kept growing. News of his lucrative business reached President Laredo Bru, who demanded a share in the profits, but Benitez refused. He had been appointed to his post by strongman General Batista himself and considered himself immune to the president's demands.

Manuel Benitez Gonzales' appointment as head of the Department of Immigration had been up to then a namely honorary nomination, since Cuba had few immigration laws before 1939. But the new decree placed him in a powerful position. One that he used to his full advantage. More than 4,000 permits were sold between January and May of 1939.

As soon as Haim heard about the permits, he saw a way out for his family. He quickly contacted Gitel and Jacob and between the three of them and the Kantors put together the

112

money needed to bring the rest of the family to Cuba. He sent the permits home and waited anxiously for news. As the days went by, Paulina came to care about Mindle, Esther and Sonia, the sisters back home, as if they were her very own, and by the time Haim, buoyed by the developments, asked her to marry him she quickly accepted.

The wedding was set for late September and in April Haim wrote home again with the news. By then Europe was facing war. The year before Hitler had invaded Austria and taken over Czechoslovakia, and in spite of the Fhurer's repeated promises not to invade Poland, Haim was becoming increasingly concerned about his family as news of the arrest and segregation of European Jews started reaching this part of the world.

By early May he had sent two telegrams with no reply.

"I should have heard from them by now. Something is very wrong," he told Paulina one night as they sat in the Kantor's living room. He had lit a cigarette and a smoky screen now stood between them.

"Could they have moved?" asked Paulina. "Perhaps they decided to leave Poland, I'm sure you'll hear from them once they're settled," she said, taking his hands in hers and moving closer to him.

"My parents are too old to move. And with me gone, the girls would never leave them. It's not like them."

"Haim. These are war times. People are forced to do things they would never do under normal circumstances. Give them some time. Maybe they're trying to get to Holland. I hear it's safer there."

She would say anything, do anything to take away the pain she saw in his eyes. But as the days went by without an

113

answer, a fine dust of despair settled around them until it became a permanent feature of their daily lives, and bit by bit they learned to live with the growing uncertainty of what was going on back home.

Rosa Olex was in the Flander's passenger list. The first of May she had posed for a picture with her niece and nephew back in Pinsk, the Polish city where she lived. She wanted to take the picture with her before taking the train that would transport her to Warsaw. From there she was to continue on to Le Havre, and sail in the Flandre to Cuba. The trip was the fulfillment of a dream. The only single girl in a family of two brothers and five sisters, she had been invited to come to Cuba by one of her sisters, who had sent her one of Benitez's permits. Rosa was only 22 when she boarded the Flandre. She had never left home before.

Once aboard it did not take her long to meet other young people. There were parties, elegant dinners, it was a beautiful ship, full of lights and laughter. She met another family that was also going to join relatives in Cuba. There were six Luskys on board and they kept an eye on her. "I'm sure your parents will thank us one day," one of them told her as they imposed a curfew for the night.

By the middle of May another letter came from Hannah. She had gotten passage for herself, Esther, Mindle, her husband and her two children on one of the German liners and they were now on their way to Havana. Sonia, the oldest, was staying with her parents, who did not want to leave. They felt they were too old to undertake such a long voyage. Instead they sold their own permits and gave that money to the girls who were sailing on the SS St. Louis. They were going to stay with relatives in Holland until things settled down.

Haim was jubilant. "They'll be here next week Paulina. That means we'll have some of my *mispocha* for the wedding. God almighty, such news, maybe things will start turning around after all! We'll have to find a place for them to stay."

It was decided that they would find an apartment for Mindle and her family nearby and Hannah and Esther would stay with the Kantors rather than in the province with Gitele. "They're going to have to meet Jewish boys," was Sara's argument. And nobody could argue with that.

It was the first time in months that Paulina had actually seen Haim happy. Sara found them a small apartment a block away from their own and Paulina went out and bought linens and kitchenware so that everything would be ready for their arrival.

"You'll fall in love with Shosh, Paulina. She'll have you wrapped around her little finger in no time. You'll see." He went out and bought a doll that afternoon. And Paulina got a new dress for Shosh and spread it daintily on her new bed. She wondered how she would get along with her new brother in law, who was the son of a big rabbi. She herself was not very religious since she came from a traditional, rather than an observant family, but brushed her worries aside and concentrated on the preparations.

By the end of May Mindle's apartment was complete. Paulina put on a new dress, checked her hair in her bedroom mirror and, with a smile of satisfaction, came down to meet Haim, who looked resplendent in a new guayabera.

"Your sisters won't recognize you," she said taking his arm

in hers, with that suntan and dressed in white you look almost like a native."

With his blonde hair and white, even teeth he looked more like a movie star from California, she thought and smiled pleased with her future husband. By the time they went down to the docks, throngs of people were already lined up at the pier. The news of the arrival of the St. Louis had spread fast and now hundreds of people were waiting. Finally the silhouette of the ship could be seen in the horizon preceded by two smaller ships, the Flandre and the Ordoñez.

On a sunny May afternoon the Flandre dropped anchor in Havana Harbor. The palm trees and the wide avenues of Havana could be seen from the ship, and the dome of the Capitolio was shining in the distance. Rosa Olex had not seen her sisters in years. She found a spot against the crowded railing and, standing on her toes and waving her arms, started screaming "Burman, Burman," calling out the name of one of her brothers in law. Three people answered. One of her sisters' husband and two nephews had come to greet her from Camaguey, a province in the central zone of Cuba, where they all lived.

As the St. Louis got closer to the docks the outline of the people leaning against the railing started to take shape and soon hands could be seen waiving frantically as Paulina and Haim strained to see if they could recognize anyone among the hundreds of faces on the side of the ship. Finally Haim shouted "Mindle, Itzhak, here, here," as he took Paulina by the waist and directed her attention to starboard.

"There, there," he shouted signaling to a man, a woman with a baby in her arms and a little girl that were now frantically waving back. "Haimele, Haimele," they shouted, "soon, soon", as the man lifted the girl who was throwing kisses in the wind.

The ship came no closer than about ten feet from the docks and suddenly several Cuban officials came on board. One of them demanded to see the captain.

The New York Times edition of June 3, 1939, published the story of the 907 refugees that were not allowed to disembark in Cuba. A rumor that the U.S. would accept them was started on board in order to avoid a mass suicide.

Left: Rosa Olex, second from left, second row, surrounded by the Lusky family in front of the hotel in Nantes, France, where they waited for the telegram that would allow them to return to Cuba.

Below: Officials abandoning the St. Louis. Courtesy Yad Vashem

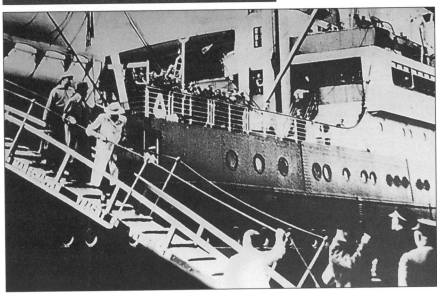

7

THE ST. LOUIS

-News of the forthcoming voyage of the St. Louis was received with satisfaction by Jews around the world. The Joint Distribution Committee announced that the Jewish Relief Committee in Havana would aid in the settlement of the refugees, and made that fact known to President Roosevelt's Advisory Commission on Refugees. But the Joint paid little attention to a cable received from its Havana representatives announcing Decree 937.

The new Cuban law was carefully studied, however, by London's Intergovernmental Committee on Political Refugees established at the Evian Conference of 1938. The Committee cabled Hapag House, the main office of the German line, advising them that great difficulties could arise in regard to the Jews entry into Cuba. Within hours of the departure of the ship, on May 13, the Ministry of Propaganda in Berlin disseminated stories that the passengers of the St. Louis "were fleeing with stolen hoards of money and much else." These communiqués were quickly picked up by the Cuban newspapers, inflaming popular opinion against the refugees.

On May 26 1939 Cuban Secretary of State Remos wired the captain of the St. Louis refusing landing permission. The following day the ship dropped anchor just outside Havana Harbor with close to a thousand Jewish refugees from different parts of Europe. Two workers from the Jewish Relief Committee who had come to welcome the refugees were detained by a police captain and a detachment of patrolmen, on their way to boarding one of the launches that were to approach the boat. They were told that only the twenty-two passengers with proper Cuban visas could come ashore. The rest had all sailed with Benitez's special permits which the Cuban government now declared invalid and demanded $500,000 in order to allow the refugees into their country.

For three days the ship idled a few feet away from Havana. On the third day Rosa Olex's brother-in-law came on board. He was escorted by a Cuban official. "Don't worry, you're coming down, everything's arranged," he told her in Yiddish. But another passenger overheard the conversation and dennounced her to the captain. Rosa had to stay on board.

For three days Haim and his family came to the harbor, looking out to catch a glimpse of his sisters, who waved frantically from the side of the ship. Esther, the youngest, leaned against the railing extending her arm as if to touch her loved ones at the pier.

At that moment one of the small launches which carried a group of government inspectors was getting ready to sail towards the St. Louis. Before anyone could stop him, Haim jumped in and in his broken Spanish pleaded to be allowed to see his family.

"Do you have any sisters, officer? " he asked.

"Do I have any sisters?" asked the man surprised by the question. "Four no less, and none of them married!"

"Then I beg you to let me see mine," answered Haim.

"*Déjalo*," said the man, after he recovered from this impromptu approach. "Let him be."

Haim was the first to jump out once they reached the big transatlantic and frantically went looking for his family. He found them sitting on a bench on the upper deck, where Shosh was playing with another little girl. When she saw Haim she jumped up at him and put her arms around him. "Haimele, Haimele," she shouted, "you came for us, you're taking us with you, aren't you?"

"I will darling, but not yet," he said handing the little girl the doll he had bought for her weeks before and taking her in his arms while he covered her with kisses. "There are still some papers to be filled." The rest of the family had now surrounded him, covering him with kisses and embraces and wanting to know the news from shore.

"Haim, will you be able to help us?" asked Hanna, taking Haim's hand in hers and giving it a big squeeze, while Mindle showed up proudly her growing belly.

"I hope it's a boy this time," she said looking lovingly at her husband. "Itzhak will be so happy! I hope he can be born in Cuba. He will be the first Cuban Morgenstern," she said referring to her husband's family name.

"Maybe he'll grow up to be a rabbi, like my father," said Itzhak, while Haim tried to hide his growing concern as he joked around with them. He stayed for another hour, until the officials came back for him announcing that the launch was leaving and everybody that was not a passenger had to abandon the ship. Haim hugged and kissed everyone, promising that they would soon be reunited in Havana. Tears were clouding his eyes as he jumped into the launch and waved back to his family on board.

On the way back to shore his mind was racing, shuffling the alternatives that were still open. The Jewish Relief Committee, the local politicians, perhaps even the press. He would exhaust all avenues, he promised himself, Shosh's face still fresh on his mind. That little girl has to have a chance, he kept saying to himself, she has to have a chance...

One of the Jews at the pier on the day of the arrival of the St. Louis was Morris Landau, a comfortable industrialist who had made a small fortune in the garment business in Havana. After the refugees were not allowed to disembark, he went back to his comfortable Vedado apartment and started pacing the floor, looking at the photographs on the wall. There were pictures with friends at outings and parties, of his young daughter and son... Landau was at the forefront of the Zionist movement in Cuba and worked tirelessly to help Jews emigrate to Palestine. It was as if by so doing he was paying back for choosing to emigrate to Cuba instead of following his early dream of building a Jewish state in Palestine. But his older brother had sent passage to Poland for him to join him in a small town in the Cuban province of Las Villas, where he had originally settled and there had not been too many doors open at the time. By becoming a Zionist leader he lived vicariously the life he had dreamt of, surrounded by people who shared his idealism and who had also worked hard and prospered in their adopted country.

They had worked with the zeal of immigrants who had everything to gain from their efforts and within a few years they had dominated the apparel market. By the late 30's Jewish firms accounted for 60% of all shoe, clothing and fabric production on the island. With little commerce or industry unrelated to sugar, the country stood in need of an entrepreneurial class and the Jewish workers, unable to survive in any other way, stepped gingerly into that role, becoming businessmen instead. Businessmen who, like Landau, could now afford to help other less fortunate Jews.

Sheina Landau came into the apartment and looked thoughtfully at her husband as he paced the floor of their living room.

"Morris, what's wrong," she asked as she stepped in from a trip to the market, setting down two packages for the young maid to take to the kitchen.

"The President has denied entry to the St. Louis. He won't let the refugees land."

"But why?"

"The officials at Hamburg-American Line claim all permits are in order, but the Cuban government says Benitez's documents are not valid and suspended the salaries of twelve diplomats and consuls for having issued illegal permits.

"Apparently some Cuban official got rich on the misfortune of these poor people and now they won't even let them land," he said pounding his fists on a delicate rosewood table.

"What will happen to them Morris?" she asked, getting closer in order to stroke his dark, closed-cropped hair. He was the love of her heart. When she first saw him at a party at the Centro Israelita she had not been impressed. He had dark good looks and black eyes that burned with purpose, but he was short and dressed like a country boy. However, when he first talked to her she could not stop listening. And she had not stopped listening ever since. They had been married for four deliriously happy years. When she looked at him now she could see that burning that she knew so well reflected in his eyes once again.

"What do you think? They'll be sent back to Europe and put in concentration camps to rot away. We can't let this happen to them Sheina, not if we can have any part in this. We can't..."

She had seen him like this before when, as a young leader of the tailor's union he had led a strike that had changed considerably the conditions of Jewish skilled workers in Havana during Machado time. President Machado had instituted a rule of terror and pledged to a program of reform that included martial law and the prohibition of street peddlers. As a result Jewish peddlers were arrested, which led to the creation of trade unions. The 1930 labor laws that required at least half of the employees of any Cuban business to be Cuban nationals, compelled many Jewish skilled workers to emigrate. Those who remained were forced to become independent tradesmen who worked under contract for large manufacturers. Some, like Landau, eventually ended up with their own businesses. Perhaps it was time to galvanize the Cuban Jews once again, but this time for a far different reason.

"Morris," said Sheina getting even closer, "you're right, we can't let this happen. But you can't do it alone. You must talk to other people. Now you are just an angry voice, but if you get all the Jews in Havana together you will make a much louder noise. They will have to listen to you. Go out, gather some friends, get some strength on your side. You have done it before."

"I'm not as young as I used to be Sheinele, do you think they will listen?"

"If they don't listen to you, who do you think they will listen to? A man they don't know and don't respect? I'm proud of my husband and there's not one Jew in Havana who doesn't feel the way I do."

"Now tell me, what would I do without you?" he said affectionately, taking his wife's face in his hands and kissing her lightly on the lips.

"Go now Morris darling," she said stroking his face tenderly "and may God be with you."

He worked hard and swiftly, gathering signatures and talking to everyone he knew until the small community had been mobilized in a common effort. When he had enough names he called on Batista who, as a strong promoter of business and entrepeneurship was known to sympathize with the Jews.

The Cuban strong man listened to his plea and promised to talk to President Bru as soon as possible, but as the hours and then days went by without an answer, Morris realized that the situation called for a different line of action. One of those who came to his aid was a young Polish refugee. Haim Tuchman had a vested interest in the St. Louis. Three of his sisters were on board.

Together they called on the Jewish Relief Committee in Havana, but the Committee was only set up to help once the refugees had landed. However their efforts did not turn out to be altogether fruitless. After a long conversation the JRC offered to contact the Joint Distribution Committee in New York. The JDC in turn sent down Lawerence Berenson, a lawyer and an experienced troubleshooter who, as a former

President of the Cuban Chamber of Commerce in New York was also a personal friend of Batista.

Morris Landau and Haim were now sitting at a cafe with Berenson. A few drops of *cafe con leche* had spilled on the small table as they finished their morning coffee and the waiter cleaned it up promptly with a rag as he took away the cups.

"*¿Otro cafe?*" he asked looking curiously at the three men sitting on the cane and wood chairs who talked in a strange language he could not understand (actually a mixture of Yiddish and English)

"*Sí,*" said Morris, "*un cortadito para mi, por favor.*" From where they were sitting they could see the outline of the harbor and the Malecon, washed out in the distance by the white light of early morning.

"Mr. Berenson," Morris was saying excitedly in Yiddish, "you have to use the full weight of your authority. President Bru has to understand that these are human beings. Under no circumstances can they be allowed to be sent back to Germany, surely they will be killed."

"I will try Mr. Landau, believe me. I haven't come all this way for nothing. I'm confident that President Bru will listen to our appeal. He seems like a reasonable man," answered the lawyer who, as a seasoned negotiator had seen many situations like this come to a head before. "Be patient, everything will be resolved, but you are going to have to trust me."

By Thursday, June 1, Berenson met with President Bru who agreed to accept the refugees if the Joint Distribution Committee posted a bond of $453,000. Berenson was only authorized to spend $250,000. Negotiations were going to be difficult. On June 2nd the St. Louis sailed out of Cuban waters to wander in the Caribbean while Berenson continued to negotiate with Cuban officials.

A few days later word went out that the captain feared a collective suicide attempt if the refugees were forced to go back to Germany —including the 250 women and 200 children on board. The day before the scheduled sailing relatives and friends circled the boat on small crafts exchanging letters, straining their eyes to see the figures at the rail.

That same day a German lawyer by the name of Martin Loewe slashed his wrists in front of his family and jumped overboard. He was saved by one of the ship's sailors and taken to Calixto Garcia Hospital in Havana where he was declared in critical condition and allowed to stay until he recuperated from his wounds.

"I did not expect you to land this way in Cuba," said Haim trying to make light of the nightmarish situation as he put his arms around the unfortunate refugee who stared at him in disbelief from his hospital bed "We'll do everything we can to keep you here. You just get well."

Loewe was pale from the blood loss, but managed to ask: "How... how is Leah?"

"Your wife and children are well. We succeeded in sending a message to her on board telling her that you were all right and were staying here for the time being. We are still trying to get the States to open the doors and there are a couple of other countries that we're negotiating with. Don't you worry. Something will turn up. It always does." Then, searching into his pocket he took out an orange. "Here, let me peel this for you."

Everyday Maximo and Haim would visit Loewe at the hospital and every day they would plead with the authorities to let him stay. But the official position never wavered. He was to be deported back to Germany as soon as he was well enough to travel.

With negotiations at a stallmate, John L. Lewis, leader of the Intergovernmental Committee on Refugees in London sent this telegram to Batista:

"I beg to take the liberty of making a personal appeal to you in the name of humanity to permit the landing in your country of the desperately unhappy refugees now on the steamer St. Louis. These refugees, if returned to Germany, will undoubtely be sent to Nazi concentration camps.

"I take the liberty of appealing to you because of your well-known feelings for the victims of German Nazism. I do hope that some aid can be given to these victims."

Batista never answered.

On June 6 the St. Louis and the Flandre weighed anchor as refugees thronged to the rails and waved frantically to family and friends along the sea wall as the vessels negotiated the channel and sailed past Morro Castle into the open gulf. The ships halted twelve miles off Havana in a last effort to wait for the outcome of Berenson's negotiations. Haim's family was still on board the St. Louis, the outline of Havana's skyline still visible from their spot on the railway of the majestic liner. Rosa Olex and the Luskys were on the Flandre, still waving to their families ashore, when twenty launches filled with port police and marines escorted the ships from the harbor and a short distance beyond Morro Castle in order to prevent any passenger from jumping overboard.

Berenson went back to New York and Landau, Haim and

THE ST. LOUIS

Maximo Kantor stood at the pier watching the diminishing outline of the St. Louis and the Flandre as they dissapeared into the horizon. The ships sailed within view of the Florida coast, but the United States would not allow them entry. Neither did Jamaica nor the Dominican Republic. In the end, four countries took in some refugees: Holland, Belgium, England and France, where the ships stopped for a few days before going back to Germany.

The St. Louis touched first on the port of Veracruz, Mexico, where some passengers who had proper visas disembarked, before sailing back to Europe. The Flandre stopped in Port-au-Prince, Haiti, where Rosa Olex saw a man "the color of charcoal" and she thought he was going to stain the white shirt he was wearing— she had never seen a black man before.

Upon their arrival in Nantes, France, the passengers of the Flandre received further instructions. They had three days for their families to cable a guarantee that would allow them to return to Cuba. Rosa told the officer she had no family left in Pinsk. She knew that if she went back, they were going to kill her.

That same day when she returned to her hotel room there was a cable waiting. She opened the envelope and sat down slowly on the side of the bed before starting to read the letters pasted on the yellow piece of paper. They were writen in Spanish, but she could make out the words "Cuba" and "*garantía*". Jubilant, with her safeconduct in hand, Rosa said goodbye to the Luskys, who were still waiting for news from Cuba, and went straight to the train station, where she bought a one-way ticket to Paris. Once seated in the train compartment, she took out a piece of writing paper and started to write a letter to her mother. Whatever happened, she wanted her to know that she was going back to Cuba, and to safety. But no matter how hard she tried, the words would not come. Instead tears started to flow. First they were just a trickle, then they became big salty drops that fell on her maroon wool coat, leaving wet patches wherever they landed... until she found herself wracked by sobs she could hardly control. She had suddenly realized that what she was about to write was a good-bye letter to her family back home. She crumpled the piece of paper, opened the window and threw it to the wind. She was not ready to say good-bye, not yet. "I'll write from Cuba," she thought, "when I have an address they can answer to," and concentrated instead on the bright summer landscape that laid out before her, as the train sped through the French countryside.

Her thoughts turned to her visit to the Cuban Consul. Would he give her the visa? Certainly her papers were now in order. Then an alarming thought crossed her mind. What if he asked her for money? She had just enough to buy another boat fare, and this time it would have to be steerage! She brushed that thought aside and closer her eyes. At her age, Rosa was not an overly religious woman, but she found herself pondering what special favor from God had singled her out from all the other passengers of the Flandre to be able to return to Cuba.

The next morning, as she looked for a taxi at the exit of La Gare, the Paris train station, her old fears crowded her chest once again and she hoped the driver that finally stopped in front of her wouldn't hear the crazy beat of her heart as she lugged her small suitcase into the seat and asked to be taken to the Cuban Consulate.

An hour later she found herself facing the Cuban diplomat, but the memory of her previous sailing came back to haunt her and she started to shiver when she walked into his office. "Tell her to quiet down," the consul said through an interpreter. If she has any problems getting on board, I'll go in with her," and he put the official stamp of the visa on her passport.

The wedding plans went on as scheduled and in the early part of September Paulina set out with Sara to buy the material for the wedding gown. Paulina had wanted to see every single piece of lace there was in Havana and they started early to take advantage of the morning shopping before the stores closed for lunch. The bus let them off at Drogueria Sarra. You could find almost anything in Havana's oldest and largest drugstore and Paulina loved to get lost in the aisles full of toiletries imported from Spain. Colognes, soaps, perfumed talcum powder, lined up in neat wooden shelves next to toy trains, doll houses and kitchenware. They browsed for a while and finally settled on a bar of fragrant sandalwood soap which the attendant wrapped in a piece of shiny brown paper.

They walked the rest of the way through narrow cobblestone streets past Compostela and Aguacate. It was only ten o'clock in the morning when they got to Muralla Street, the hub of the fabric stores in Old Havana. Their first stop was at a friend's store.

"*Mazel tov!*" cried out Sender Rabinowitz when he heard the news. "So we'll have a wedding soon. You did well coming in. I have the best lace in all Havana. French, no less. It's becoming harder to come by with what's happening in Europe, you know..." he said lowering his voice.

Sara looked at Paulina with concern. She knew the war was

a delicate issue betweeen her and Haim. They had received no news from his family since they were sent back to Europe. They still held the hope that they could have been taken in by England or France, but as time went by that possibility became more unlikely. The only thing keeping them from total despair was that Poland was not yet at war.

Paulina remained impassive and asked the man to bring down a delicate white Chantilly and a rich ivory Alencon. The choice was difficult, since both set out Paulina's face to perfection.

"They're both beautiful, aren't they?" said the storekeeper, and he cut out two samples from the heavy bolts of lace that were sitting on top of the counter.

"Here, take these out in the daylight so you can appreciate them better," he said to Paulina as he pointed to the sidewalk.

She took the two samples in her hand and was standing near a newsstand looking at the lace when a headline in the morning paper caught her eye. She crossed the street to the small stand, oblivious to the lottery vendor who insisted on selling here a lucky *billete*. Still holding the samples she handed the attendant a ten cent coin and bought the paper. Her hands were trembling when she came back to the store.

"What is it child? What happened? You look like you've seen a ghost!" Sara took the newspaper from Paulina's hands and tried to steady her as she read the headlines.

Hitler had invaded Poland. Europe was at war.

"It says here that Jews, gypsies and other non-arians are to be sent to labor camps," said Paulina while tears flooded her eyes. "Oh mother, what will happen to Haim's family?"

Sara put down the newspaper on the store's counter and held her daughter in her arms.

"Be a good wife to him darling. Give him your love. That's all you can do. He needs you now more than ever."

"Hannah wanted so much to see America. Oh mother," cried out Paulina "she's only seventeen! And those two babies...Oh God, how do I tell Haim?"

8

A TIME OF DISENCHANTMENT

We never heard from my father's family again. And even though we expected the worst, the confirmation of their fate came after my father sent a cable home saying that he had gotten married and never got an answer. After that my father never spoke another word about Poland or his family. The little that I know about them I heard from my aunt Gitel, who kept pictures of my grandparents and of my father's four sisters. He never uttered another word in Polish. It was, in essence as if that part of his life had never happened.

He embraced his new life with renewed fervor and whatever dark memories festered in his heart were replaced with an irreverence that included an infectious sense of humor and a complete disregard for religion. As far I can remember he never again set foot in a synagogue. "I can't believe in a God that allows things like that to happen," he would answer whenever we would prompt him to go to *shul*, referring to that darkest moment of his life.

Tradition became relegated to my grandparent's home, where we would celebrate Jewish holidays. On Passover seders we would congregate around my grandmother's table for a feast of chicken soup with *kneidlaj*, roast veal and scrumptious Passover *kugels*. But I couldn't wait for Passover to come to try some of her *teiglaj*, the traditional sweets that she kept in a jar dipped in honey. She would only make them for Passover and would take them out at the end of the meal one by one, the honey shining like liquid amber that I would lick before putting the delicious confections in my mouth.

It was there that I learned about Eliyahu Hanovi and the cup that we would leave full of wine for him, and whenever us kids were not looking my grandfather would shake the table to pretend that the profet had taken a sip before hiding the *Afikomen* for my brother, my cousin and I to find.

I must say that whatever sense of tradition and Jewishness I have was instilled in me mainly by my grandparents.

My grandfather turned a new leaf when he came to Cuba. His gambling was restricted to a tame game of cards with friends. He was a gentle man who loved nature and I realize now that the lushness of Cuba must have been for him a tremendous source of pleasure. He converted the patio in the back of the store into a big aviary by covering the whole thing in metal mesh and there he would keep dozens of tropical birds, from the tiny *toti* to *sinsontes* and canaries that delighted us with their beautiful singing every morning. My grandmother on the other hand derived her pleasure from cooking, which she did as if she were still in the old country. Her home-made farmer cheese was prepared by filtering a quart of unpasteurized milk (the only kind we had) into a small sugar sack and letting it drain overnight. In the morning when we came into the store we had a beautiful fresh chunk of farmer cheese which we ate by itself or on a piece of rich dark bread.

As to my father, he kept his disenchantment deep inside. For his friends, Jaime Tuchman was a *simpatico* character, always with a funny story and a smile on his face. He succeeded moderately in his business, but for him, having seen how precious life can be and how soon it can end for some, enjoying it came first. He became an ace domino player and he could be found every weekend on the second floor of the Casino Deportivo, our beach club, playing dominoes in the big airy hall that overlooked the ocean, telling jokes to his steady entourage of friends and aspiring players who would congregate around him to watch his moves and learn from the master.

My father enjoyed his work as much as the rest of his life. He always carried a piece of candy in his shirt pocket for the pretty shopgirls when he visited the department stores, where he found himself almost every day calling on department heads to show his samples and get approval for his orders. He had realized long before that retail was too slow and the hours too long for him and had taken a bold decision to start manufacturing ladies lingerie. The beginning was difficult. He struggled for a while selling to the shopkeepers he already knew, until one day he decided to make a few special samples and approached the three major department stores in Havana. "All I need is three good clients," he told us. "If I can get El Encanto, Fin de Siglo and La Epoca, I'll be in business."

Funny enough the first one to open the door just a crack was the biggest. El Encanto placed a small order of petticoats. This was in the early 50's, when the flare skirts with pom poms that were all the rage required supporting undergarments to keep them afloat. (They were supposed to stay up, which was gravitationally impossible). My father designed a petticoat with several layers of tulle in a rainbow of colors that resembled the inside of a can-can skirt. The top was plain, but when you lifted it you were surprised by rows and rows of tulle in the most beautiful colors that made the widest skirt stay up. The stiffness of the tulle did the trick. Tomas Menendez, the Director of Advertising of El Encanto, was the one that came up with the name, and the can-can petticoat was all the rage that summer of 1952. I had one made especially for me with an extra row of tulle that came up almost to my ears whenever I sat down, but it also showed up prettily whenever I crossed my legs or bent even slightly. Who would have thought that our fortunes would change because of a petticoat!

Soon after, the other big stores followed suit and my father's new business was under way. But most importantly, Tomas Menendez and him became good friends. A Spaniard and a Jew united by mutual respect and a strong sense of ethics. "We do business on a handshake," my father used to say. "I trust that man with my life." They would meet over drinks at the Cafe Encanto to exchange jokes, smoke cigars, look at the pretty girls and enjoy the scene of Old Havana.

Saturday nights I would watch my parents get all dressed up and step out with several couples for a night of dinner and dancing at the famous Tropicana nightclub, where statuesque mulatto girls would dance on platforms set out on the branches of huge tropical trees. On cold nights a glass ceiling would close in mechanically over the huge open patio and the show would go on, still under the stars. There was also the

Montmartre, the Sans Souci and later on, the fabulous casinos of the Riviera, the Capri and the stately Hotel Nacional, with its elegant terraces overlooking the Malecon and the waters of the Atlantic. There in balmy nights, you could sit in huge rattan chairs and enjoy a *mojito* while listening to a band play the dreamiest of music under a velvety sky. These were the days of Benny More and Olguita Guillot, Cuba's musical icons that created some of the music we still love, boleros and ballads that can evoke a whole different mindset by the sole magic of their melody. These were also the days of Nat King Cole, who paid frequent visits to Tropicana, where he held the audience in rapture with his unforgettable voice.

In the early 50's Havana became a favorite playground of stars like Errol Flyn, George Raft and Frank Sinatra, who could be seen sipping *daiquiris* at the Riviera and basking in the sun poolside at the Nacional. Unfortunately, being so photogenic and having so much atmosphere, it did not take long for Havana to be chosen as a second Las Vegas by the American gaming lords. Meyer Lansky made it its second home when he opened the ritzy Capri Hotel, which rivaled the Riviera with its leopard-print carpeting and crystal chandeliers. The buzzword was opulence and no expense was spared in making Havana a top contender for Las Vegas and even Miami Beach. This was a game that was being played wholeheartedly by Batista and one that brought increasing tourism— and dollars— to the country.

Things couldn't be better. And things couldn't be worse. A revolutionary leader by the name of Fidel Castro brought in a new ideology that spread the gospel of reform to the *campesinos*, the poor farmers that toiled the countryside and lived humble existences at the fringes of the wealth that was being enjoyed by the business people, the cattle and sugar lords and the industrialists.

The *campesinos* never starved. The Cuban soil is too prodigal for that, but their lives where mired in illiteracy and Castro promised equality for all and death to yanqui imperialism. Appropriately, he hid in the mountains of Oriente province, deep into the Cuban countryside, where he slowly gathered a band of loyal supporters. The *barbudos*, who grew a beard like his as a symbol of rebellion.

Batista's government answered with a strong repression. Dissidents that were apprehended were tortured and killed. Students rioted at the university, which was closed half the time. Consequently those who could afford it sent their sons and daughters to study abroad, but my father wouldn't hear of it.

The repression we lived with filtered down to our social life. Young people were not allowed to go out in groups to the beach or to the country for fear of being apprehended on grounds of conspiracy. There were so many acts of sabotage that the government took no chances. Violence became a way of life, and Batista's G-2, the repressive arm of the police, bloodied their hands repeatedly trying to put a stop to the mounting insubordination. Once, while riding a bus on my way to the University of Havana, a barrage of bullets forced all the passengers to get down on the floor. The police was fighting with the students in plain daylight. Some boys were killed that day. It was always the students who protested, the ones who had the most to lose seemed to be the most willing to risk their young lives for an elusive chance at freedom.

9

THE CAPRI

The comptroller of the Capri Hotel woke up with a bad headache. It was bad enough that he had Meyer Lansky for a boss. Him he could handle. It was easy. As long as the numbers were up there, Lansky was happy. And the numbers had not disappointed him so far. Attendance at the casino was at an all-time high and the hotel was booked solid for the New Year holiday. Yes, 1959 was going to be a banner year. But what got Leo Rosen rattled was what he had seen just the day before at breakfast time. He had come into the hotel cafeteria to show Lansky the latest figures and he had actually seen the old man get up to salute a stranger. He was almost standing at attention in front of a burly dark-haired man with a bad attitude.

For Lansky to get up and practically curtsy in front of somebody, that somebody had to be someone special. Rosen did not have to wait long to find out the identity of the dark stranger. The hotel was buzzing with the news of his arrival. The man was none other than Santos Quatro Terra. The mafia strong man had actually come to Havana and Leo better had good figures for him — he tought, or else. Perhaps he had seen too many mafia movies, but the whole situation of his employment was beginning to make him feel uncomfortable.

Rosen was extremely bright, with a good head for figures. But his real talent was his ability to cozy up to people in high places. That was what had landed him his position at the Capri, but he wandered now about the merits of his good fortune. What good was it to make a high salary —paid in dollars, not pesos— if his life was at the mercy of these mafia characters. Even the slightest error could have major consequences, perhaps not fatal, but.... Leo started to perspire even in the freezing room kept cold by central air conditioning. Anyway, he reminded himself, the hotel and the casino were a huge success, he had nothing to worry about— for now.

He opened the door of his wood-paneled closet and chose a dark suit. December, January and February were the only months when he had a chance to wear the slightly heavier suits he had bought in New York before graduating from N.Y.U. and coming back to Havana. He liked the professional look they gave a man, and gave himself an approving look in the floor-length mirror that lined the closet door. He turned around, took his crocodile leather briefcase and proceeded to the elevator of the Focsa building where he pressed the first floor. Soon he was walking out of the elegant lobby to his car that was parked discreetly in a side street.

It was January 1 and none of the office personnel was working, but he had some figures to work on for the next day and wanted to be prepared. As soon as he put the small dark-blue Ford in gear he noticed more people than usual in the street, particularly at this early hour after a night or partying. He himself had gone to bed early. There was nobody special in his life at that moment and he didn't see the benefit of staying up all night and waking up with a hangover. For the time being his time was better spent at work. There would be plenty of time to party... once he got to where he wanted.

His parents had worked hard at the fabrics store to pay for his education in the States and now that he was on his own they enjoyed a comfortable life in one of Havana's seaside suburbs. But he wanted more, much more. His years in New York had given him a taste for luxury, and expanded his awareness of the things money could buy. He enjoyed walking down Fifth Avenue and looking at the store windows where one could find everything under the sun, from Italian suits to the finest French shirts and smooth leather attachés. He enjoyed the feeling they gave a man. He would always live in Cuba, you could not beat the lifestyle, but he promised himself that once he made his money he would shop in New York.

Now that he was working at the Capri he had seen the American tourists that stayed at the hotel and the kind of money they threw every night at the casino tables. The beautiful women they came with, the jewelry, the furs... he wanted to be able one day to spoil a woman that way. And he had the smarts —and the perseverance and work ethics to get there. He knew he would get to the top. It was only a matter of time...

As he turned the corner of the Malecon to get to the Capri he saw a parade coming down the street and slowed down to get a better look. The men walking by were dressed in olive garb and sported long beards. They were being followed by a long line of people, who jumped in from the sidewalks, some throwing flowers at them and shouting "Revolución, Revolución!"

"My God he did it!" he thought, as he rushed to the hotel, "Fidel came down from the mountains." He parked his car in the employee lot and went up to the executive offices. Lansky was sitting in the lounge with the dark man. They were smoking cigars and watching the news on television. Batista and his family had fled in the middle of the night. Castro was now in power.

"It's all over kid," said Lansky as he put out his still smoldering cigar in a big crystal ashtray. "We have nothing else to do here. We're going back home and I suggest you do the same if you want to have a future."

"You mean you have nothing to do with the hotel any more? Just like that?" said Rosen leaning against the door frame.

"Just like that kid. You can't run a casino with revolutionary types running around the streets. Besides, you'll see, it won't be long before they take over all the hotels in Havana. This is beginning to smell like a commie job to me."

"But Mr. Lansky, if that's the case then I'll be working for the government..."

"That's just it, kid. But I don't think you'll end up with a good pension in this case. If you know what I mean..."

The dark man patted Lansky loudly in the back and started to laugh. Rosen turned around and ran in the direction of his office, but it was locked. He tried his key but it did not work. Someone had changed the lock overnight, which meant the papers with the latest figures were probably in someone else's hands. Maybe Lansky himself had done it in preparation for what he saw coming, maybe the revolutionary chiefs had gotten their hands in themselves. At this point he did not really care any more. All he wanted was to get out of there.

He went home and called his father.

"Dad, it happened. Fidel came down from the mountains. You better make arrangements to leave."

"We know Leo, we've been watching the news on television. He has quite a following. What's your rush? Let's see what he does first. He has to be better than Batista..."

"Dad, don't bet on it. I've heard some alarming news at the hotel, from people who know a lot more than we do. I'm telling you, things are not going to be good."

"So go to New York for a few weeks, you have friends from college. Ask for time off from work. After all, you have not taken a vacation since you started working. It'll do you good son..."

"It's not that easy Dad, I can't just ask for vacation now. It will look suspicious. But I'll find a way. I don't want to stay here, and I don't think you and mom should either."

"Don't you worry Leo, we know how to take care of ourselves."

Leo Rosen looked helplessly at the telephone in his hands before putting it down in its cradle. "Stubborn people," he said and turned on the television.

The next morning as Rosen was coming out of the shower, he received a telephone call. He was being summoned by the new manager of the Capri and was to report to him within an hour. He dried himself up and wondered what he would want to see him for. "I hope he does not want to promote me," he thought, and chuckled at the irony of the situation as he chose a maroon silk tie and a pair of dark gray gabardine pants that he wore with a white poplin shirt before slipping on a navy blazer. He got to the hotel and went straight to the office of Augusto Sierra.

Until the day before Sierra had been the Assistant Manager in charge of night operations, and Rosen used to run into him all the time on those occasions when he worked late, which was often. As a result he was a witness to Sierra's frequent indiscretions. His last involvement had been with a young reservations clerk who had quit the hotel a month before from one day to the next, without any notice. They were about the same age, and as co-workers they had been at the same level, with Rosen pulling a slightly higher rank as comptroller, but now the tables had been turned and he found himself looking at his new superior across a big glass-topped desk.

"You know Leo, I have always had tremendous respect for you. You have done a wonderful job for the Capri and I expect you to keep doing it now that the hotel belongs to the Revolution," Sierra started to say, turning the big leather chair where he was seated to look directly at him.

Rosen felt his chest tighten at the mention of the word "Revolution". He had come to the meeting with a different agenda. Not thinking that things would be moving this fast, he had wanted to submit his resignation, but now as a de-facto government employee in a high position his situation was much more delicate. To resign could be seen as a counter-revolutionary act, and punishable by incarceration. His mind raced for an alternative. He was street-smart enough to realize that he needed some leverage on his side in order to come out with a smooth solution, for he did not relish the thought of working for Castro's government and even less, to linger in a Cuban jail.

Suddenly he remembered the night clerk and he sent an unspoken prayer to the pretty girl. His face muscles relaxed. She was going to be his ticket to freedom. He took a deep breath and said:

"Augusto, whatever happened to that cute reservations clerk you used to hang around with? I always thought it was strange that she disappeared from one moment to the next. I thought it was even stranger that there was money missing from petty cash all of that week, and the following two weeks after her departure. Would you say it was coincidental, or perhaps the young lady needed some assistance to get her out of an embarassing situation? I have the figures to prove it, you know..."

Sierra's expression changed from one of placid condescendence to one of surprise and then outright fear. His hands were gripping the sides of the big desk and Rosen could see his right leg beginning to twitch.

"What do you want Leo?" he finally asked.

"I want you to fire me."

The next day Leo Rosen was on a plane to New York.

10

EL ENCANTO

The Advertising manager of the most expensive department store in Havana was in an uproar. In the twenty years since Tomas Menendez had been in business he had never been so frustrated. And justly so. This time of the year he always started getting the latest fabrics from Paris and Milan so that his top designer could put together the fashions that would grace the windows of El Encanto in time for the busy Christmas season.

But this year he would have to make do with whatever he had in stock. He pondered this last thought for a moment, adjusting his black-framed glasses. To be fair, that was plenty. His stockrooms were full from frequent buying trips to Europe but still, his customers demanded the very latest. The display windows of El Encanto were changed like clockwork and Havana women looked forward to this weekly event. The ones that could afford to, bought the creations that Antonio would whip up in his salon; the ones who could not, picked them up from the racks of the fashionable store at lesser prices. Those who could do neither would buy the fabrics and rush to their dressmakers to copy the styles. But one way or another, El Encanto set the fashion trend for Havana and Tomas Menendez felt responsible.

The store's ads were as slick as Madison Avenue's and his business took him often to New York. But lately imports had been severely restricted, and when his last trip had to be canceled for lack of dollars, he saw the handwriting on the wall — and he did not like what he saw.

Tomas Menendez had come to Cuba from Spain as a youth, and worked his way at the store to the top. At middle age he did not fancy starting all over again —and where could he go? Go back to Spain? Luisita, his young Cuban wife would never want to leave her family. In the ten years they had been married they had accumulated a large circle of friends and his two kids loved to spend summers at the beach, where every year they would get nut brown under the hot Cuban sun.

Luisita was fifteen years younger than him and beautiful. She had smooth olive skin and dark hair and was slimmer than most Cuban women. He had spotted her among the salesgirls that stood at the entrance of the store selling cosmetics and married her when she was only eighteen. Now at twenty eight she dressed with the distinction of the young Cuban matrons. You could see her most of the time in a linen shirt dress and a simple strand of pearls. But then she didn't need much more to look spectacular. She was the love of his life and he indulged her in every way he could, and her frequent visits to the store gave him tremendous pleasure.

He reached out for the box of H. Upmanns he kept in a corner of his desk and took out a cigar. He smelled it, luxuriating in the pleasure of the aroma, clipped one end and lit the other, as he twirled the cigar between thumb and forefinger. He inhaled deeply, appreciating the smoothness of the leaf. Nothing relaxed him more than a good Cuban cigar. And God knew he could use some relaxation these days.

I was now a senior in college and was looking for an internship. My father arranged a meeting with Tomas Menendez and in early March I put together a few samples of my work and headed downtown for my first job interview. I went into El Encanto and took the elevator to the fifth floor, where I had so often visited with my father, only this time I was alone. I walked up a short flight of steps into the mahogany-paneled reception area. The walls were lined with newspaper clippings of fashionably dressed models, stamped at the bottom with the signature logo of the store, and I became overwhelmed by the glamour of my surroundings. The world of fashion always intrigued me, and El Encanto was the place were style was crafted in Havana, a veritable temple to elegance and good taste. All my instincts told me that this was where I wanted to work.

A recepcionist greeted me with a polite smile and asked me to sit down before disappearing behind the maze of hallways that laid beyond the wood and glass door at the back of her desk.

A knock on Tomas' office door made him look up. Reina De Armas, the Director of Advertising walked in, taking him away from his thoughts.

"The new trainee is here. I thought you might want to meet her," she said opening the door and letting herself in.

"Bring her in Reina," he said putting out the cigar reluctantly on a huge onyx ashtray he kept by his side.

I walked in and waved my right hand instinctively to clear up the odor of tobacco.

"I apologize for the smoke," said Tomas, "I had just lit up a cigar before you came in."

"That's all right, my father smokes them sometimes and I usually react the same way whenever he does," I said smiling, trying hard not to offend him.

"Please sit down," he said and motioned to a black leather chair in front of his desk.

"Your father and I have been friends for a long time. He tells me you can write copy. Is that true?" he asked, looking at me appreciatively.

"I think so Mr. Menendez. I'm an Advertising Major at the University."

"But if you're still in school..."

"Classes are only offered at night," I blurted out, "and I have too much time in my hands. Besides," I added, regaining my composure, "I think that working will help me learn faster."

"Why El Encanto?"

"Mr. Menendez, I love this store. Ever since I was a little girl my mother would bring me shopping with her and later my father would take me to see his merchandise displayed here. I was so proud to see his designs in your ads. I promise I won't disappoint you."

"Do you have a sample of your work?"

I opened the briefcase that had been sitting on my lap, produced a short manuscript and handed it to Tomas. He took it hesitantly, but as he started reading it I could see his expression start to change from one of condescending curiosity to one of surprise and finally of pleasure.

"This is very good," he said handing the paper back to me. "Your writing has a spark. I think Reina could use some help. When can you start?"

"How about Monday?"

"That sounds good to me."

"Well if that is all, I won't take any more of your time, Mr. Menendez," I said putting the manuscript back in the briefcase and closing it shut.

"Wait a minute, don't you want to know the salary?"

"Oh yes, of course," I said turning beet red. I was so excited at being allowed to write El Encanto's advertising copy that I forgot I was going to get paid for it on top of that.

"You'll start with $85 a month as a trainee. If everything is fine we'll give you a raise in six months."

The money wasn't much, even for Havana's standards, but if he only knew that I would have done it for nothing.

"That's fine Mr. Menendez. That's just fine," I said getting up and shaking his hand awkwardly, and left before he could see the huge grin that had already started to spread on my face.

Despite the confusion that reigned in the country, I was happy with my work. I was assigned the Saturday page and was in charge of gathering merchandise from all the different departments that would be featured in the ads and later allowed to write some descriptive copy. As a result I became familiar with the ins and outs of the store, which occupied a whole city block at the corner of Galiano and San Rafael, in the center of downtown Havana.

El Encanto brought in exquisite merchandise from Europe and the States and when the revolution came, it held supplies that could have lasted for another five years. Silks and brocades from France, exquisite laces from Spain, shoes from Italy. The spoiled ladies of Havana had their pick in that store. The style was mostly European, since we followed Paris and Milan more than New York, but the advertising style was strictly Madison Avenue and I thrived surrounded by all that creativity.

I enjoyed being called into the Salon Frances, the designer room, to see a new bride being fitted. I was in charge of naming the new creation and writing a piece for the social pages of *El Diario de la Marina*, the right-wing newspaper that would later publish a photo of the bride.

As my ability to write copy improved, I was gradually allowed to write bigger pieces, until I was finally entrusted with a complete fashion ad. I still remember the feeling when I saw it published in the morning paper. I had decided to work on a new concept and discussed it with Raul, the fashion illustrator, who drew up two models facing each other, in a way that you could barely see what they were wearing. The copy was laid out in the middle of the page with the headline: "It's time to face change... the new look is here!" and underneath in small letters: "...come see it at El Encanto." The next day there was a line of women waiting for the store to open.

Tomas usually communicated with me through Reina, but that morning he stopped at my desk. He tapped his fingers on the desktop and simply said: "Well done." Coming from him it meant: "Wonderful!"

11

A RENDEZVOUS WITH DESTRUCTION

It was particularly warm for October. A most unwelcome fact after a long, hot summer. But then, that year in Havana nothing seemed to go right. For the most part of the morning the phones had not been working. I looked at my watch and walked away nervously from the bedroom window. Downstairs, the neighbor's children were waiting for the school bus, their navy and white uniforms a sharp outline against the green manicured lawn. It was one-thirty. Noon break would soon be over. I picked up the phone and tried the call again. This time it went through and I held my breath. A woman's voice answered.

"May I talk to Alex?" I asked, my heart pounding.

"Señor Alex isn't in," the voice said indifferently.

"Do you know where he is?" I insisted.

"He didn't say miss. I must go now."

"Wait." Don't hang up. Just tell me. Is he all right?" I pressed on.

"I can't say anything miss," the voice answered curtly. "Good-bye."

Damn that stupid maid! At least I was quite sure nothing really bad had happened. That much she would have told me, I thought with relief. He was probably hiding. That morning a French freighter had been blown up to pieces, its load of ammunition igniting the sky like a stream of firecrackers in the morning sun. The explosion had taken place at the harbor, a good ten blocks away, but the impact had been strong enough to rock the fifth floor of El Encanto.

I had stayed a little longer after lunch break had been called in order to finish some ad copy and had been alone in the office when it happened, barely missing the fragments of glass that had shattered all over my desk, leaving a trail of dust and debris wherever they fell. I had finally quieted down long enough to look out the broken window. The big cloud of smoke that had started to rise in the horizon was coming from the waterfront and I wondered if the Americans had finally come.

"Perhaps the madman is right after all and we are being invaded," I thought and turned on the radio to listen to the news. The La Coubre had been transporting Belgian ammunition to Cuba when it had exploded. There were over fifty dead and close to two hundred wounded. There was suspicion of sabotage. Certainly the numbers were impressive, but not much more than the daily toll of casualties that by now we had all gotten used to hearing about. For the last two years we lived with constant rumors and haranguing speeches, and after a while one adjusted.

The announcer warned people to stay away from the harbor, for fear of a second explosion. I couldn't imagine how anyone in his right mind would want to go down there. As I gathered my things and headed for the door, he was blaming the Americans for the death and the destruction. I turned off the radio and walked away. Lately, Americans were being blamed for everything...

I brought myself back to the moment, leaned closer to the mirror that lined the bedroom wall and dabbed some gloss on my lips, put on my shoes and headed for the door. The iron railing felt cool and hard under my hand as I stepped on the rich mahogany stairs which now gleamed in lazy patterns in the bright noon light, and I was suddenly filled with a sense of comfort. I always liked that time of day when the smells of the kitchen mixed with the warmth of the day to give the house a cozy, homey feeling that made me feel especially cared for. I could almost hear my father's words as I reached the landing. "Never take what you have for granted. For us it wasn't always this way," he would often tell me. I had grown up acutely aware of my surroundings, as if having been born on this side of the world was some special gift that God had inadvertently bestowed upon me.

"Betty, where are you? the car's waiting." My mother was standing at the front door, her bright yellow cotton dress a sharp contrast to suntanned arms as she carried a bunch of freshly-cut roses from the garden.

"I'm coming mother." I was almost running now, the clip clop of my heels resounding noisily on the tiles of the long hallway.

"Be sure to be home early tonight, Grandpa Maximo and Grandma Sara are coming over for dinner. You know they don't like to eat late, and please don't go out of the store."

"I should be back by six," I said, ignoring her last comment, I was not planning to do anything but get back on the car and come straight home after work, anyway. I planted a kiss on my mother's cheek and rushed out the door. "Tell father that Tomas wants to see him if you talk to him."

A light blue Chevrolet was waiting at the curb, shaded by a flowering royal poinciana tree, its fiery blooms beginning to form an orange blanket on the ground after displaying the last colors of the season.

"Had time for a little siesta?' asked the driver, sitting up as I opened the door and settled in the back seat. The velour of the seat felt soft against my hand, and as I ran my fingers against the material Alex's face became etched on my mind. How long had it been since I'd last seen him? Two, three weeks now?

"Not today Ramon," I answered, coming out of my reverie. "Any news about the speech?"

"No, only that it will be tomorrow at five. Mariana invited the neighbors to watch it on TV. You know how excited she gets every time Fidel speaks," he said, putting the car on gear.

Ramon had been with my family for years. He ran errands for my mother and took my father and myself to work every day. In exchange he received a small salary and knew he could count on us for any emergency. His was a simple life, and he liked it that way.

But his wife had different ideas. Ever since Castro came to power she had become an ardent supporter and a member of the militia that stood ready "to defend Cuba against imperialist aggression."

"It is your duty to join the militia," she would often tell her husband. But Ramon Suarez was a stubborn man. Mariana was entitled to her ideas but nobody was going to tell him how to dress —and even less make him carry a rifle. Besides, he would rather have a beer with the guys in the *bodega* than God forbid... march!

I nodded and wondered whether Alex's disappearance had something to do with this morning's incident. Somehow he always seemed to be ahead of things, as if a sixth sense guided him. "The mystery man," my mother used to call him.

The car turned into a wide avenue lined with majestic royal palms, their heavy fronds fluttering in the breeze and Fifth Avenue, the main road of the seaside suburb of Miramar now stretched out before us as we drove into El Vedado, past elegant apartment buildings, parks and movie houses on our way to downtown Havana.

Twenty minutes later we could see Morro Castle, the lighthouse by the harbor, jutting out of the Atlantic where the seashore met the Malecon, that wide promenade populated by ice cream vendors, children with their nannies, tourists and lovers looking for sunshine and ocean breezes. In the distance, merchant ships and cruise liners found their way to Havana Harbor where the debris from the La Coubre was still being cleaned up. We drove on the far side of the boulevard, trying to stay as far away as possible from the harbor, while seagulls pirouetted against the blue sky, dotted here and there by soft cotton clouds, and I wondered how an act of violence could take place in the midst of so much beauty.

On this particular afternoon there were still no signs of the slight change in the air that heralded the mild Cuban winters and as we drove away from the seashore and into the narrowing streets of the business district, I felt increasingly warm in the back of the car and leaned against the open car window. The exhaust fumes of the buses made me suddenly nauseous. I closed the window, leaned back and thanked God the ride was almost over.

Outside a row of storefronts was still covered with rolling metal shutters, but as opening time approached, shop owners began rolling up the shutters with long metal sticks, revealing thick rolls of material, ribbons and lace.

Refreshed by the midday sojourn, they now readied their wares for the busy afternoon trade that would soon animate the narrow cobblestone streets.

As we approached the store from San Rafael Street I could see that some of the display windows had been changed. Every year, like clockwork, on October 14, the salesgirls would start to wear black, the store windows would show the new collections and "winter" would officially arrive at El Encanto —no matter how hot it was outside. This time the windows were covered with huge sheets of blue and brown paper in anticipation of the unveiling of the new Dior collection as I walked through the stone portico that stretched through the length of the store.

A steady stream of passersby were leisurely strolling, stopping every now and then to say hello or pat someone on the back. In fact perhaps more business was conducted here or more formally across the street at the Cafe Encanto, with its French parlor white marble tables and wood and cane chairs than in any other place in the city. It was often said that if you wanted to see anyone in Havana, all you had to do was stand in the corner of Galiano and San Rafael and sooner or later you would run into him —or her.

A RENDEZVOUS WITH DESTRUCTION

I went up a side entrance and took the elevator to the fifth floor where the advertising offices occupied a good third of the floor. I greeted the receptionist, who waved absentmindedly as she carefully retouched her lipstick and went through the maze of dark wood and glass partitions to my cubicle in the back, just opposite the office of the head copywriter.

Reina de Armas looked up from the layout she was studying and smiled looking at my flushed face.

"It's much too hot in October to start wearing black!" I complained, fanning myself with a magazine. "I wish they would not make us stick to that silly rule. We're not salesgirls, for heaven's sake, we work at the Advertising office," I said.

"I know", said Reina, "I've talked to Tomas many times, but its easier to convince a Spaniard to give up his wine than change a rule."

At thirty five, the only daughter of one of Havana's foremost journalists, Reina de Armas was in charge of all the copy that appeared in El Encanto's ads. But more than that, she was entrusted with something far more delicate —the advertising style that carried the store's trademark: a blend of Paris and New York chic coupled with a dash of tropical nonchalance. A style that had taken almost a century to develop and by now had become second nature to the store's employees.

Part of it was due to El Encanto's ironclad rules, like the need to have summer and winter uniforms. And over the years Reina herself had acquired that special style that comes to women of a certain class. She played with a strand of pearls that graced her simple black linen dress, and asked me if I had turned in the copy for the Saturday ad.

Unfortunately I was still waiting for the clothes, since the

163

department managers didn't seem to be able to make up their minds about which dresses to run. "They have trouble with deliveries," I told her.

"I know," she said, playing with a pencil, "lately everybody seems to be waiting for something. We don't seem to have enough of anything."

It occurred to me that it would be a good idea to stock up on white material. "You could always make sheets out of it and if need be it could be died any color," I told Reina, "my aunt told me that people used to do that during the war."

"I would have never thought of that," she said, looking at me with renewed interest. "I've always admired you Jews. You seem to have a sixth sense for facing trouble."

"It's called experience," I said, straightening up in my chair. I had never felt obvious antisemitism. Cuban society was far too open for that, but all the same, the word "*Judío*" still made me cringe.

"By the way, how's the fashion show coming along," she asked, anxious to change the subject.

"Ask Antonio," I answered, motioning to a thin, bespectacled man dressed in black gabardine pants and a white, impeccably pressed poplin shirt that was fast approaching us. He was carrying two oversized fashion sketches which he held up to us.

Few people could find their way around the stockrooms of El Encanto better than Antonio Dominguez. As the store leading fashion designer he knew of every piece of fabric that came in from Paris and where perfect accessories could be found to complement each dress. His guidance had proven invaluable to me during the past year.

"Who thought of having the girls carry the sketches?" I

asked him, in an attempt to cheer him up, since he seemed rather downcast this afternoon.

"Who do you think?"

"Maria Baron, I assume." He nodded and lowered his voice to a whisper before adding, "between you and I, she told me it was her farewell gift to the store. They're going to have to find a new fashion director. She's moving to Florida. I understand she has an uncle in Clearwater."

"Clearwater, where is that?"

"Somewhere in the west coast of Florida," he said and drawing closer he added in a conspiratorial tone, "things are no good Betty, have you thought of leaving?"

I looked at him worriedly. Everybody talked of leaving these days. My father had mentioned it the night before over dinner and I wondered whether my grandparents' visit had something to do with that. Grandpa Maximo seemed to be always there when important decisions had to be taken. He had been there when they had decided to move to the new apartment and it had been him who had finally convinced my father to let me travel to the States the summer before. But I did not want to think about that, not yet anyway.

The winter show was the main event of the year and customers came from all over the island to watch the collection and put in their orders well ahead of the busy social season. Normally the whole designer floor was taken over for the fashion show, but this year they had gotten less responses than usual and only three rows of chairs had been positioned on both sides of the passageway, leaving an aisle on which a wooden platform had been raised. Now the lights had been dimmed and the models pranced around the platform in crisp linen and silk creations on which

Antonio had implanted his unmistakable seal of understated elegance. The theme, carried over from the display windows, was *Cafe Royal*, a symphony in browns and blues; the colors indicating the season, since fall barely came to Havana and women remained faithful to silk and linen, leaving the colors to echo the changing mood of the North.

"How's it going Antonio?" I asked as I saw the designer making notes behind the scenes.

"I'm not sure Betty. I have less clients, but the ones I have are buying more than ever. It's almost as if they were afraid we were going to run out of clothes. Señora Menocal ordered the midnight blue chiffon and Amelia Carreño wants the linen chemise in brown and white. We're going to need twenty yards of pearl-embroidered Alencon lace from France for her daughter's wedding. I hope we get the material on time. It's going to be the party of the season, Betty. Eight hundred people at the Havana Yacht Club." And then, getting closer he whispered: "too bad the girl is not much to look at, but by the time Miguel gets through with her at the Salon, she'll look like an absolute angel."

Yes, I thought, everything was going on as usual. There was still time...

12

WHEN OUR LIVES TURNED

The table was set when I came home that evening and the minute I saw my grandmother putting the last touches on the setting, I knew that something good was cooking in the kitchen.

"Abuela, you made *blintzes*," I said hugging my grandmother and planting a kiss on her cheek.

"And how do you know *sheine meidele*?"

"I can tell. I can tell by the look in your face. Did you fill them with the cheese you make?"

"Yes," she laughed heartily, and her ample bosom went up and down, "I made them just the way you like them."

"Mm... Abuela, you're great. Where is Grandfather?"

"I believe he's talking to your father in the terrace. Come sit with me and tell me about your day. How's it going at work?"

I started telling her about my day at the store when suddenly the aroma of frying food wafted into the living room and I went into the kitchen to steal one of the cheese-filled crepes that the maid was just then taking out of the frying pan.

Julieta our maid was a tall, heavyset mulatto that intimidated almost everyone. From the grocer to the fruit vendor she would get the best produce —or else. One rotten *malanga* or a tough piece of meat and she would take her business elsewhere. But not before she would give the unfortunate man a piece of her mind.

The kitchen was Julieta's domain. She kept the white tile floors and light wooden cabinets sparkling. But my father was not allowed in. "You mess everything up señor Jaime," she would say. "If you want anything, ask me. I'll bring it to you."

The only one who could get away with anything with Julieta was my brother Michael. She would spend hours sitting on the floor of the kitchen playing Parcheesi and Monopoly with him and she would laugh and laugh whenever she caught him cheating, which happened all the time.

The only other mortal allowed in the kitchen was my grandmother. Abuela Sara's cooking was the glue that held the family together. Her *cholent* cooked all day Friday for the Sabbath meal. The dish, which originated in the frozen *shtetls* of Europe, was a rich stew of meat, beans and potatoes. Far too heavy for a midday meal, particularly during the hot Cuban summers, but the tradition was kept at lunchtime every Saturday —rain or shine— followed, invariably, by a round of siestas.

Abuela Sara's love of good food reflected in her countenance. A happy woman who had remained oblivious to the pounds that had crept up on her over the years, her milky-white skin had not lost the radiance of youth, and she wore her shiny gray hair tied back in an elegant bun.

"Come here, naughty girl," she said to me, shuffling her

heavy frame in the living room sofa. "You're not supposed to eat those before your dinner."

"Oh Abuela, how do you make them so good? Are you going to teach me one of these days," I asked, sitting down next to her in order to feel her pleasant warmth, taking a bite of the *blintz* which I had wrapped neatly inside a paper napkin.

"As soon as I can get a hold of you for two whole hours," she said as she gave me a quick hug.

There were voices coming out of the terrace. The heavily-accented one belonged to Grandpa Maximo, a short, frail looking man in his late sixties, with wire-rimmed glasses that rested on top of a strong nose.

"Hola Abuelo. What were you and papi talking about so secretly?" I asked.

"We'll fill you in after dinner, not now," said my father, "I'm hungry. Come on, come on, we'll wait for you while you wash up," he said.

"Yes father, "I said, walking towards the bathroom. "I missed you at the store today." I opened the water faucet. " I thought you had a meeting with Tomas."

"We met in my office," he replied curtly turning in the direction of the dining room.

I washed my hands and splashed some water on my face before joining the others at the big dining room.

"Julieta made arroz con pollo tonight," said my mother who had come back after peeking in the kitchen to check if dinner was ready. "And we have fresh mangoes for dessert. Would you believe there are still some around in the middle of October?"

"Thank God!" I replied, "That must be the only thing we are not short of."

"Shush," said my mother giving me a meaningful look. "Julieta could hear you. Her boyfriend is in the militia."

"So what, she's the first to complain when we can't get beans and rice. I'm fed up with all this hush hush business," I replied and hurried to find my seat at the table.

My mother looked at my father, who brought a finger to his lips motioning her to keep quiet.

Dinner was served every night in a spacious dining room that overlooked a downstairs yard planted with neat rows of jasmine and gardenias, and the heavy scent of the flowers wafted in now through the grillwork of the open window and drifted in with the evening breeze.

The maid brought in a big platter of yellow rice with pieces of chicken laid out in the middle and decorated with red peppers and green peas. Another platter of fried bananas laid by its side.

"I hope everybody is hungry," said my mother as she started serving. We ate in silence for a few minutes, except for my bother who was playing hide-and-seek with the maid.

"We're inaugurating a new campaign," I said to my father to break the silence brought up by my outburst. "I'm sure Tomas filled you in. I think he wanted one of your night gowns for Saturday's ad. I hope you'll be able to deliver. I spent all afternoon trying to round up enough merchandise."

The plates were cleared and coffee was served.

My father brought up a cup of thick black coffee before answering, his eyes fixed on the design of the delicate porcelain. "No darling," he said, after emptying the tiny cup. "I don't think I will be able to deliver. I'm having trouble getting material from the States."

Why is that? You never did before," I said, alarmed at what was now obviously becoming a national malady.

"The mills are tightening my credit. They're worried I won't be able to get the dollars on time."

"But you always paid them before. My God you've been doing business with them for over twenty years. They ought to know you're good for the money."

"If I were in the States I'm sure I wouldn't have a problem Betica," he said using the Spanish diminutive as a sign of affection. "But the political situation here has them scared."

"I guess they're not the only ones," I answered, pushing away a plate of fruit. "I hear Maria Baron is leaving the store. She's going to Florida. What are we going to do papi?"

He was looking steadily at me, his usual sparkling eyes now clouded with concern.

"We're going to have to find a way to get you out of here until things quiet down. I don't like the idea of your working at a big store like El Encanto. The government may take it over any time. It's the logical step after nationalizing the banks.

"But father, that may never happen. You said yourself the Americans would never allow it. And I love my job. Reina de Armas told me only yesterday that I was in line for a promotion." I was looking at my grandfather as I spoke, praying silently for his support.

"I hear you were caught downtown in the middle of a bomb scare this morning, Betica," Grandfather Maximo said, barely raising his voice. "This time nothing happened to you, but what if it does?" His fists were now tightly closed on top of the table, betraying his usually placid manner.

"Havana is no longer a place for a young girl like you.

Believe me, I've been here for over thirty years. I've seen good times and pretty awful things in Cuba and I have a feeling that what we are about to see will top them all."

"But Abuelo, I don't want to go. I don't want to leave all of you and besides, where am I going to go?" I was looking at each one of them, asking for reassurance, but I could tell from the fixed expression on their faces that it was going to be difficult. Finally I looked at my father, sensing my defeat.

"I've already made arrangements with aunt Bess in Miami," he said, referring to my grandfather's sister who owned an apartment building in Miami Beach. "She'll be expecting you in a month. Until then you are to go to work every day as usual. No need to arise suspicions."

That night I heard from Alex. "Hi Betty," he crooned into the telephone nonchalantly, "I've missed you."

"You could have fooled me! I thought I'd never hear from you again," I said and a tone of resentment crept into my voice. I hadn't heard from him in a week.

"I've been in hiding."

"Why. What did you do?"

"We were going to plant a bomb in one of Fidel's depots, you know, where he stores his ammunition, but someone blew the whistle and Alberto and I had to leave for Matanzas early in the morning, not even my mother knows where I am. I'm staying with a family that belongs to the movement. Thanks to them they didn't kill us. But by the time I get back to Havana my bags will be packed, if you know what I mean."

"I know, they want me to leave too. What do you think will happen now?"

"I'd say sit still Betty. I think the Americans are going to get involved. There are rumors that they are already training some people in Central America. It will take a while, but they will have no choice."

"What about your family Alex, are they leaving too?"

"I want them to leave. I think things are going to get worse before they get better. I already told my father to get some money out of the country and get out of here for a while, but I don't know if he'll listen. The old man is tough, you know, but my brother's got his ear and is trying to convince him to buy new machinery in Italy for the factory. He even got a special letter of credit from the Department of the Treasury. He's very close to the minister."

"I hope your father will listen to you. It would be madness to invest money in machinery now," I said and added, lowering my voice: "I'm gonna be leaving soon Alex, and I don't know if I'll be able to see you before I do."

"Don't worry, I'll find you," he said and the line went dead.

13

THE LAST CURTAIN CALL

The store looked strangely different that October morning.
But I felt the change even before I saw the smattering of
employees that gathered here and there in lazy chitchat, oblivious to the approaching opening time. And even before I saw
the olive green fatigues of the Revolutionary Army that now
replaced in many of the employees the usual black uniforms of
the winter season.

Crazy, I thought, but then, everybody seemed to prefer to
dress that way these days and yet I couldn't help thinking that
the grand old store seemed stripped this morning, like a lady
that has suddenly been caught off guard without her makeup.

I walked by the jewelry department, where I usually stopped
once a week to see what new pieces I could pick out for the
Saturday ad, but as I got closer I realized that some of the trays
were being put aside by two employees and a uniformed guard
was counting them and putting them away in a big metal box.

I looked away and kept on walking, but felt strangely violated, as if part of me had been put away in that metal box against my will. I had to reach Tomas Menendez's office, somehow he would explain everything to me.

I kept on walking, avoiding the stares of the guards, looking for the elevator that would take me to the Advertising office, past the accessories department, the rows of imported silk scarves and leather belts neatly lined up at either side of me. As I approached the end of the floor I noticed that some of the men were carrying rifles, a challenging grin now replacing the solicitous smile of the sales clerks. I recognized some of the faces. One of the women lived close to me and I used to give her a ride home every now and then. On the way we used to exchange store gossip and confidences about boyfriends. She looked at me once and then avoided me. There was nothing else to say. There were obviously some unspoken issues we had never discussed before and about which we were now at terrible odds. Her world and mine were about to collide, and hers seemed to hold much more weight than mine right now. I felt strangely intimidated and tried to shake off the feeling of helplessness that was beginning to take a hold of me. "This is where I come to work every day," I told myself. "There is nothing they can do to me. I am an employee, just like them." I knew that everything would be all right once I reached my office.

I was walking faster now, my steps matching the crazy beat of my heart and got into the elevator just as the doors were about to close. I stepped in quickly and looked around; there were only three other people with me, two men and a woman. The woman and one of the men were in uniform. The other man, who was older, was wearing a dark blue suit and was smiling sadly at me. After a few minutes I recognized him. He was one of the department managers that I used to collect mer-chandise from.

"I have to reach Tomas Menendez's office," I was muttering softly like a comforting litany over and over again. "He will explain, he will explain everything." I got out of the elevator and turned right towards the hallway that led to the execu-tive offices.

"Hold it, nobody's allowed in here," I heard a familiar voice from behind the glass doors as I started to push them open. The voice had the slow inflection of the *guajiros*, the Cuban peas-ants. A young boy no more than sixteen stood guard with a rifle. He was waiting alone in the reception office, his small frame dwarfed behind a huge mahogany desk.

"Let me in, Juan," I ordered the young messenger boy. "I have to talk to Tomas." I remembered the first day he had come into the office. He had been very shy and had hardly talked to anyone, but Tomas had taken a liking to the young *guajirito* and had given him a job while he paid for his schooling in the city. Now the uniform bolstered his confidence and he looked me straight in the eye.

"Sorry Betty," he replied, a cocky smile illuminating his pubescent face, "from now on you're gonna have to talk to me. Mr. Menendez's office has been taken over by the Revolutionary Army. I'm the *camarada* in command."

I hesitated for a minute. My world was crumbling fast and I was trying to grasp at the pieces left. I took one more look at my cubicle, where I had taken my first incursions into the world of writing and ideas. My eyes rested for a moment on the newspaper clippings that were hanging on the wall of the reception area, the sleek illustrations outlined crisply against the columns of copy and I felt the familiar rush of excitement at seeing my work on the printed page.

I murmured a silent good-bye, turned around and retraced my steps. I started running towards the elevator but decided to take the stairs instead. I ran down, the sound of my hurried steps echoing in my ears as I left the fourth floor, and then the third behind me. I stopped for a minute to catch my breath when I got to the third landing, but heard voices near the door and started running down again. This time I didn't stop until I got to the bottom and, pushing open the heavy metal door that led to the main floor, walked out, past a group of employees that were lining up in front of a table that had been placed in front of the escalator. Someone was taking down names.

I was almost running now, trying to contain the panic that was spreading through my chest; my cheeks felt flushed and I started to become dizzy, but I knew I had to keep going. I had to get out of there, into the fresh air of the morning, because it was becoming increasingly difficult to breathe where I was. I was about to get to the door and out into the street that was beginning to fill up with early shoppers and busy business people when a hand held me firmly.

As I turned around, I heard a man's voice. "Aren't you gonna sign up for the militia?" Omar Hernandez, the Assistant Manager of the men's department had always been extremely polite whenever I had come around looking for merchandise for the Saturday ad, almost to the point of flirting. Only he wasn't flirting now. His hand held my left arm firmly as he looked me in the eye. "Why are you still wearing black? You should be dressed in olive green fatigues like the rest of us," he said.

I felt a fury rise in me and shook myself free with a sudden jerk of my arm that caught him by surprise.

"Let me go Omar," I said, "I'm not joining any militia or the union for that matter, I work at the Executive Offices and my loyalty remains there."

I had raised my voice and curious shoppers and other employees had started to crowd around us.

"You shouldn't talk like that Betty, you could be blacklisted if you don't join the union, you know that. Every worker has to belong. There are no two ways about it."

"I don't care about your black list. I'm not one of you, and I don't give a damn who knows it. Let me go!" I was shouting now and working my way swiftly through the crowd, disappeared into the bright October morning.

14

DEJA VU

The next day I woke up with a crushing headache. I stayed in bed most of the day and ate very little. The plantation shutters in the bedroom had been left half-closed to keep the bright sunlight out and the air conditioner was whirring softly in the background. A dresser with a big mirror that we had bought just a year before stood in front of me, the reddish mahogany of the wood catching the rays of sunlight that were filtering in through the few open blinds. "Handsome piece of furniture," I said to myself. It went with the four-poster bed that I had fallen in love with the minute I had laid eyes on it. It had not taken much to convince my father to buy it for me on the spot. "Funny I should be thinking about something like that at this moment," I said to myself.

Around noon my mother came into the bedroom.

"Want to talk?" she asked, sitting on the edge of the bed in the darkened room, and I felt her hands warming up mine. She let go of one of them and started stroking my hair, as a tear rolled down my cheek. I hid my head on the pillow to avoid her stare.

"I don't belong here anymore," I said finally, turning to face her. "I feel so strange wherever I go."

"I guess your father was right after all. As much as I hate to see you go," she said taking one of my hands in both of hers. "It will be safer if you stay away until things quiet down. I hope we're not separated for long though. I couldn't bear to be away from you," and she brushed my hair back with her hands to plant a quick kiss on my forehead before running out of the room. In her own quiet way she had always been there for me, listening to my teen-age laments, encouraging and spurring me on all my dreams, no matter how far-fetched. She was my closest ally and my most understanding friend. How would I get along in a strange country without her?

Visions of sunny afternoons strolling with my mother down the Paseo del Prado, or lost in the intricate web of the streets of Old Havana came to me, and my eyes set on a picture that stood on top of my dresser which showed a five-year-old girl dressed in a checkered jumper and a white blouse, hand in hand with a dark-haired woman with big sunglasses. That day my mother had bought me a thin gold chain that I still wore around my neck, from which hung a delicate star of David encased in a half moon. I felt the cool metal of the chain against my skin and shuddered. The warm cocoon of my existence was unraveling right before my very eyes and there was nothing I could do to stop it. My beautiful home, the warmth of my mother's love, my work, my friends, all were coming to a sudden halt.

That night when my father came home he went straight to my room. He took me in his arms like he used to when I was very small and held me close.

"It doesn't feel good. Does it darling? We're living in a crazy world."

I buried my head in his chest, smelling the familiar scent of his cologne. Every year for Father's Day I would go with my mother to the House of Guerlain on the Paseo del Prado to buy my father a big bottle of Blue Ribbon Cologne and for years I would associate the limey scent with everything manly and good. Now I wanted to take that smell with me, to saturate my senses with his presence, for I had no way of knowing when I would see him again.

He pushed me away to look at my face and smiled a sad smile. A smile I had seen only on occasion. "Little girl, look at me", he said, and his brown eyes, that looked so much like mine, looked straight at me. "I was as old as you when I came here. I had nothing, went through some very hard times, and now, just as I was beginning to make it the rug has been pulled out from under my feet once again." I thought of the stories I had heard, of the struggling years, even the times when I knew that we were just getting by before the slow-coming years of prosperity, when the stores he supplied finally opened up and showered him with orders, orders that he now could not fill. I held on to him, feeling his sadness, wishing that I could make everything right, like he used to do for me when I was small, and tried to hold on to the comforting strength of his arms around me. "I haven't told this to your mother yet, but I guess by now she has figured it out. It's going to be hard for her, we both worked hard all these years, but I don't think we'll be able to stay here. Believe me, at my age I don't relish the thought of starting all over again, but what else can I do?'

I felt salty tears brushing down my lips and wondered when

I would hear my father laugh again, tell his usual jokes. It had been weeks since I had seen him smile and realized now how difficult it must have been for him to urge me to go.

"You can't stay here Betty. After what you've done it's downright dangerous. You openly defied the regime. Tomas Menendez called me before leaving for Spain. By now everybody knows your name at the store. It's only a matter of time before they come for you. The only way for you to stay is to join the militia." He held me for a very long time while I kept quiet. I realized now that there was nothing for me to fight for any more.

"Betica," he said finally, "I love you more than anything in the world. That's why I'm sending you away. Aunt Bess will be waiting at the airport. We'll follow as soon as we can. The business cannot be salvaged, but I'll stay to see if I can get some money out of the country, even if it is at black market prices. We have no other choice."

Thus were twenty five years wiped out in a single moment. Good and bad years, but productive, solid years in a country that we considered ours. Twenty five years before, my father had made a decision. A decision that led him to set down roots in Cuba, to marry and have children, to embrace the customs of that country, to make that soil, that language, those people his very own. And he had embraced it all with the exuberance of his young years, spurred on by a terrible tragedy that had brutally cut him off from so many of the people he loved. He had turned his back on Europe to trust his tropical America and now, halfway through his life, had to pull up roots once again. It was difficult for me, but how painfully hard it had to be for him!

DEJA VU

The next day as I waited for my flight at Rancho Boyeros. Airport I realized for the first time what a strange mix I was. My ancestors were Polish and Lithuanian immigrants; through my veins ran Jewish blood; I had been born and raised in a Spanish tropical island and was now on my way to North America.

"I wonder how it will all gel twenty years from now," I thought as I watched hundreds of anxious people being searched, hassled and moved around by the men and women in the olive-green fatigues that seemed to be everywhere now. I was leaving with two bags of clothes, some linens that my mother had managed to sneak in among my things and a box of cigars that the government allowed every passenger to take out. The box could be sold in Miami for fifty dollars. Any other valuable they found on me would have been confiscated on the spot.

A black woman in uniform pulled me out of my reverie. "We need to search you," she said sternly, taking my passport and my plane ticket with her. "Follow me please." I had heard that people were routinely searched at the airport, that's why my mother had not given me anything that could compromise me, but all the same I felt my knees begin to weaken. The woman guided me to a door guarded by a soldier. "In there," she said curtly as she opened the door, closing it behind her. There was a metal table in front of me, a folding chair and nothing else. A fluorescent lamp flooded the small room in a garish light. I felt a flush cover my face, but made an effort to calm down. I knew I was not carrying any money or jewelry with me, which was what they looked for.

"Take off your blouse," she commanded, placing my pass-

185

port and plane ticket on the table.

As I unzipped the back, the fabric draped softly down the front and I remembered that I had not taken off the gold chain with the star of David that my mother had given me so long ago. I always had it on and I brought up my hand instinctively to touch it. The woman's black eyes fixed on the star with uncommon intensity and I prayed that she would not take it away. "It's been with me forever, please..." I started to say, "it means so much..." when I realized that I had seen those eyes before, in another place that seemed now lost in eternity. It had been a long, long time since I had last seen those big black eyes. The memory of a sunny afternoon in my grandfather's terrace brought tears to my eyes. It seemed a lot farther than the fifteen-odd years that had gone by. So many things had changed since then.

"Milagros!" I shouted and her face broke into a wide grin of innocence as recognition briefly replaced contempt. Her forehead, which minutes before had been shrouded in a somber frown, was now smooth and shiny as her eyes lit up with happiness. Suddenly we were both five again and rocking in my grandfather's hammock...

But the magic lasted for only a moment before the mask of military rigidity claimed her handsome black features once again. She brought up her index finger slowly to her lips, picked up the passport and plane ticket from the table and whispered: "Good luck," before returning them to me. Motioning for me to zip up my blouse, she opened the door and shouted: "All's in order," to the soldier that was standing outside.

She escorted me silently back to the line and I saw her walk away slowly, her military gait lending a proud stance to her back.

DEJA VU

Milagros' mother had been right again. Our lives had been meant to go in different directions and I sadly realized that the gap had just gotten a lot wider. The Revolution had given Milagros a new purpose and a promise of a better future. She wanted wholeheartedly to believe that she could leave the *solar* — an opportunity to have an education, to better herself and raise her children with the promise of a better future. And she had a right to want those things, I just could not accept them at the cost of democracy and freedom. I prayed that everything Milagros wanted would come through for her. If my world was crumbling, I wanted at least hers to improve, and I said a silent good-bye to my friend. "Good luck to you too," I whispered as I saw her disappear among the crowd.

One thing I was certain of. This was a one-way trip. If ever I was to get on that plane I knew I would never see Cuba again. I was suddenly swept away by a wave of nostalgia for the country I was about to leave. I would miss the easy ways of the people, the happy rhythms of my magical land. I knew then, with a certainty born of an early wisdom that I was leaving all that behind.

But I couldn't help wondering what would await at the other side of the Florida straits. There was a whole world there full of possibilities ready to be explored, and I thought of my father and that long ocean voyage so many years before. Different place, similar circumstances, I thought. It seemed that every twenty years or so the world went topsy turvy. I asked myself whether he had had the same kind of feelings at the time. For I was sad and excited. Nostalgic and curious at the same time.

EPILOGUE

Forty years have gone by since that fateful October day when I boarded a Pan American flight for Miami. My parents stayed for another three months waiting for the American invasion that never happened and finally left the country after the fiasco of the Bay of Pigs. Since then thousands of political prisoners have died in Castro's prisons, pawns in a game that only governments can play. El Encanto was bombed and reduced to a rubble two years after I left. The government never rebuilt it, considering it a temple to capitalistic consumerism and decided to build a park where it had stood —a whole city block— instead. Imagine Manhattan without Macy's! My father got to see two grandchildren before dying of a heart attack at age 60, hardly a month after attending my brother's graduation from medical school. My mother died eight months after we took her back to Cuba for her first visit after thirty-nine years. It was a touching, but shocking experience for her. The stage of her young years now as old and deteriorated as she herself had become. In retrospect it might have been kinder not to let her see what Cuba had become, and instead let her keep the rosy memories of her youth.

I married Alex who, after making a successful new beginning in Miami, died young, leaving me to raise our two children on my own. I'm recently remarried and a grandmother of two. Despite my hardships, I have managed to live a full life in my new country, both as a writer and as a woman, and I am still in awe of the wonderful things that have come my way.

I am grateful to have had the opportunity to spend the first nineteen years of my life in a magical land that will forever touch every aspect of my life with its kaleidoscopic mix of Caribbean sensuality and Spanish honor and history.

Despite all this, I still struggle to fit the different pieces of my patchworked background in order to come up with a true identity. I will never be 100% Cuban, nor am I by any means what you might call an American Jew. Instead I am slowly coming to the realization that I am a much more complex individual for having been born where I was.

Perhaps in the next generation all the elements will finally gel and become one more piece in a huge puzzle, lending one extra dose of brilliant color to the final product that is America. And perhaps one day soon that beautiful island where I was born and its gentle people will be able to join the rest of the free world once again.

The Chinese have a curse: "May you live in interesting times". I can say that myself, and those of my generation that shared my journey have truly lived in very interesting times.